How to Solve Almost Any Problem

How to Solve Almost Any Problem

Turning tricky problems into wise decisions

ALAN BARKER

Harlow, England • London • New York • Boston • San Francisco • Toronto • Sydney • Auckland • Singapore • Hong Kong
Tokyo • Seoul • Taipei • New Delhi • Cape Town • São Paulo • Mexico City • Madrid • Amsterdam • Munich • Paris • Milan

PEARSON EDUCATION LIMITED

Edinburgh Gate
Harlow CM20 2JE
Tel: +44 (0)1279 623623
Fax: +44 (0)1279 431059
Website: www.pearson.com/uk

First published in Great Britain in 2012

Pearson Education is not responsible for the content of third-party internet sites.

ISBN: 978-0-273-77049-7

British Library Cataloguing-in-Publication Data
A catalogue record for this book is available from the British Library

Library of Congress Cataloging-in-Publication Data
A catalog record for this book is available from the Library of Congress

10 9 8 7 6 5 4 3 2 1
16 15 14 13 12

Typeset in 10/12pt Giovanni by 30
Printed in Great Britain by Henry Ling Ltd., at the Dorset Press, Dorchester, Dorset

Contents

CONTENTS

About the author

Alan Barker is Managing Director of Kairos Training Limited, a training consultancy devoted to developing people's skills in thinking and communicating. He has been training and coaching since 1989, and was an actor and director prior to that. Alan has an MA from the University of Cambridge and is a member of the UK Speechwriters Guild. He is the published author of 14 books, including *Improve Your Communication Skills, How to Manage Meetings, Creativity at Work* and *The Alchemy of Innovation.*

Publisher's acknowledgements

We are grateful to the following for permission to reproduce copyright material:

Text

Extracts from *Zen and the Art of Motorcycle Maintenance: an enquiry into values* by Robert Pirsig with permission from The Random House Group and HarperCollins Publishers.

Figures

Figures 4.1, 4.2, 4.3, 4.4, 4.5, 4.6, 4.7 from *The 7 Habits of Highly Effective People*, Simon & Schuster (Covey, Stephen R. 2004) with the permission of FranklinCovey Company.

In some instances we have been unable to trace the owners of copyright material, and we would appreciate any information that would enable us to do so.

Introduction

This is a book about stuckness, and how to escape it.

You know you've got a problem when you want to do something but you don't know what to do. That's the premise underlying the title of this book. How to solve almost any problem? Really? Well – yes, if we define a problem as a situation in which we're stuck.

But problems seem to come in so many different shapes and sizes. Deciding what to have for dinner; introducing a new product to market; solving a mathematical equation; saving a marriage: can we really think about all of these problems in the same way? Of course not. But we *can* approach them using a method that will help us identify how to think about them.

So we need to begin by defining our terms. The first important point is this: *the way we solve a problem depends on the quality of the attention we pay to it.*

And attention, by definition, focuses our thoughts in a particular direction. Defining our terms is a good way to focus our attention.

It's not just a question of *how much* attention we pay to a problem, it's the *kind* of attention that matters. Human beings differ from other animals because we can *change* the way we think about a problem. Scientists call this ability **cognitive fluidity**. Here's my second observation: *we can think about any problem in more than one way.*

And that's what this book will help you to do: think about problems in different ways.

At the heart of this book is a method that will make your thinking more fluid. I've developed the method over a number of years, helping people solve problems in organizations of many kinds. The main focus of my work has been on business problems, but I firmly believe that the method outlined in this book can help us deal with a wide range of problems, from the most personal to the most global. After all, every problem is an event in a human brain, and most human brains work in roughly the same way – more or less.

Surrounding the method, which is at the heart of the book, is a constellation of ideas. (I'll be investigating and developing some of them in my blog, *Distributed Intelligence*.) Some of the ideas are mine, but many are the brainchildren of others wiser and more knowledgeable than me. Many of those people are named in the book, but I particularly acknowledge with gratitude the inspiration I've taken from the work of Edward de Bono, Jeff Conklin, Mihály Csíkszentmihályi, Stephen Covey, Helga Drummond, Paul Ekman, Tom Flatau, Vanda Forward, Robert Fritz, Howard Gardner, Daniel Goleman, Joe Griffin and Ivan Tyrrell, Daniel Kahnemann, Hank Kahney, Geir Kaufmann, Stephen Mithen, Ulric Neisser, Fred Nickols, Vincent Nolan, Roger van Oech, Tudor Rickards, Tali Sharot, Rachel Thompson and Trevor Young. Oh, and Ray, whose ideas while walking the dogs were always memorable.

This book is for Gill and Imogen.

This is the zero moment of consciousness. Stuck. No answer. Honked. Kaput. It's a miserable experience emotionally. You're losing time. You're incompetent. You don't know what you're doing. You should be ashamed of yourself.

Robert M. Pirsig, *Zen and the Art of Motorcycle Maintenance*, Chapter 24

Chapter

1

Being stuck: what it means to have a problem

Let's begin by thinking about some problems.

Think back over the past 24 hours. Note down some of the problems you encountered during that period. Think about the problems you solved and the ones you didn't; the little problems and the bigger problems; problems that people presented to you and problems that you invented for yourself.

Go ahead, do it now, before reading on. Don't turn the page until you've come up with some ideas.

Problems I've encountered in the past 24 hours

My guess is that, whatever you noted down, you haven't mentioned a whole host of problems that you solved *without thinking about them*:

- You may have mentioned that you lost the car keys; but you didn't mention that you were able to find the sugar in the kitchen cupboard.

- You may have mentioned that you discovered a problem with your computer; but you didn't mention that you changed a light bulb.

- You may have mentioned that someone made a demand that you weren't able to fulfil; but you didn't mention that you were able to meet the demands of half a dozen other people during the day.

- You may have mentioned that you felt overwhelmed with problems at one point; but you didn't mention that you cleared the 'to-do' list with which you started the day.

To make this point, allocate each of the problems of the past 24 hours to one of the four boxes opposite:

Problems you have solved without thinking about them

Problems you have solved by thinking about them

Problems you've thought about but not solved

Problems you haven't solved, and don't know how to think about

The top box should contain the most problems – by far.

Perhaps it was hard to fill in that top box because you simply didn't *notice* most of the problems you were solving. We focus, not surprisingly, on the problems we can't solve; we tend to ignore the problems we solve very successfully.

Think back over that 24-hour period again. Ask yourself: 'What problems did I solve, which I *wouldn't* have been able to solve when I was two years old?'. In the years since you were a small child, you have become one of the most proficient and effective problem-solvers on the planet.

We should celebrate our success as problem-solvers. Human beings aren't specialized; we can't fly like eagles or swim like dolphins. It's our *versatility* – our ability to solve different problems in different ways – that makes us, arguably, the best problem-solvers on the planet.

What's the secret of your versatility as a problem-solver?

Pattern-matching: the heart of all problem-solving

Let's begin with perception. How do we make sense of the world? The simple answer is: by pattern-matching. The human brain processes information in parallel. Think of it as 'bottom-up' processing and 'top-down' processing:

- **Bottom-up processing.** The brain doesn't recognize objects directly. Different parts of the brain respond to different features: shape, colour, sound, touch and so on. The neural networks that respond to all these different features – the myriad connections of brain cells in our brains – operate independently of each other, and in parallel.

- **Top-down processing.** Meanwhile, other parts of the brain are doing 'top-down' processing: providing the mental models that organize information into patterns and give it meaning. As you read, for example, bottom-up processing recognizes the shapes of letters, while top-down processing provides the mental models that combine the shapes into the patterns of recognizable words.

These two kinds of processing engage in continuous, mutual feedback. It's a kind of internal conversation within the brain. Bottom-up processing constantly supplies new information so that we can modify our mental models. Meanwhile, top-down processing is constantly integrating incoming information into existing mental models.

Our mental models make sense of the world for us. Indeed, they *create* our world. As Joe Griffins and Ivan Tyrell explain in their book, *Human Givens*:

"These metaphorical templates are the basis of all animal and human perception. Without them no world would exist for us. They organize our reality.**"**

Where do our mental models come from? Many of them we learn through experience; some seem to be 'hard-wired' into us at birth. Newborn babies, for example, can recognize faces and expressions. They can even copy actions, sticking out their tongues when they see someone else doing so, even though they can't know what the grown-up is doing – or even what a tongue is.

The brain is always guessing when it pattern-matches. Incoming information is often garbled, ambiguous or incomplete. How can my brain distinguish your voice from all the other noises in a crowded room? Or a flower from a picture of a flower? How does it recognize a tune from just a few notes? The answer is that top-down processing filters incomplete information through existing mental models and *completes the pattern*.

Visual illusions demonstrate how the brain makes these calculated guesses. In Figure 1.1 we can see a white triangle, even though the image contains no triangles. The brain's top-down processing completes the incoming information by imposing a triangle – its best guess of what's there. (The triangle is named after Gaetano Kanizsa, an Italian psychologist and artist.)

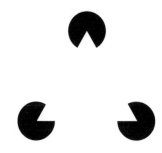

Figure 1.1 A Kanizsa triangle

This process is called perceptual completion, and it's not limited to visual information. When you hear the Beatles sing 'All You Need Is Love', it's hard not to sing the answering call ('*Da da da-da DAAAHH!*'). The moment you smell that particular scent, you're swept back to your first meeting with that special person. One sip of a Campari and soda, and I'm sitting once more on the waterfront in Venice. Perceptual completion continually helps us to create meaning from the merest wisps of information.

Ulric Neisser and the perceptual cycle

We make sense of the world, then, by matching incoming information to mental models. But pattern-matching is more than simply responding passively to incoming information. We make sense of the world because sense-making helps us to be more effective in the world.

Ulric Neisser was an American psychologist and member of the National Academy of Sciences who died in 2012. In his book, *Cognition and Reality* (1976), Neisser suggested that we use mental models (he calls them schemata) to explore the world: they act as filters through which we can select information that will be helpful to us (see Figure 1.2). A schema, says Neisser, is 'not only the plan but also the executor of the plan. It is a pattern of action as well as a pattern for action'.

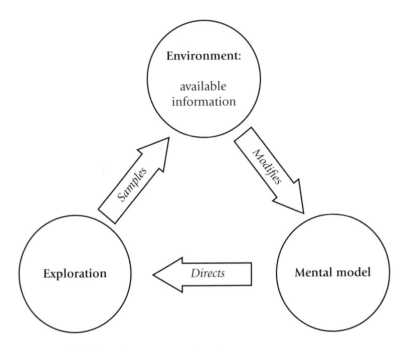

Figure 1.2 Neisser's perceptual cycle

For Neisser, sense-making and taking action are part of one continuous cycle. Sense-making begins with exploration: searching our environment for information we can use to exploit a situation to our advantage. If the information we discover modifies our mental model, we can then use the adapted model to be even more effective the next time we encounter a similar situation.

The important point is that the cycle *begins* with exploration. Our natural urge is not to solve problems, but to *look for solutions*. Every organism must explore its environment if it's to survive. The default mode of every living thing – humans included – is to hunt around in our environment, searching for information we can use to succeed.

Human beings are not so much problem-solvers as *solution-seekers*.

Intuitive problem-solving

It may not feel like it at the end of a stressful day 'fire-fighting' at work, but the history of your own success as a problem-solver is proof of this principle. Look back at that list you made at the start of this chapter: think about all those problems you solved, *without thinking about them*, as you made your way through the world.

When we're about a year old, walking on two legs is a problem. We want to get about, but we don't know how. Something impels us to try out solutions – perhaps by imitating others, perhaps by following genetically imprinted patterns in our brains – and, before long, we've solved the problem. It's the Neisser cycle at work.

As we grow up, we learn language by listening actively, trying out sounds in various combinations, monitoring the responses when we use them, and adapting the combinations. It's a process of continuous learning: we nearly all learn new words, and new ways of expressing ourselves, throughout our lives. It's another classic example of the Neisser cycle.

And we solve a host of other problems in the same way. From catching a ball to holding a conversation, from learning to whistle to maintaining a friendship, the problem-solving process tends to be the same. Encounter the problem; try out a solution; monitor the results; understand the problem more fully; try another solution. (See Figure 1.3.)

We could call this intuitive problem-solving. Intuition operates without conscious or deliberate thought. When we solve problems intuitively, we do so *without thinking*.

Intuitive problem-solving is characterized by three key principles:

1. Making sense of the problem (by pattern-matching) *always* dictates a solution.
2. Solving the problem always means *doing something*.
3. Solving the problem is also simultaneously a way of understanding the problem better.

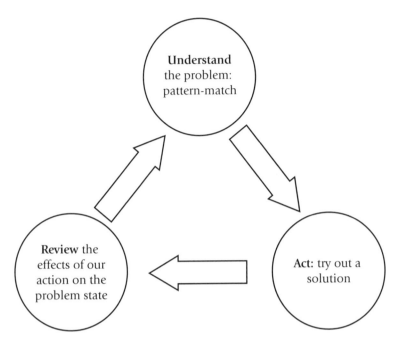

Figure 1.3 Intuitive problem-solving

In other words, in intuitive problem-solving, understanding the problem and solving it *are the same thing*. Intuitive problem-solving always combines the problem with the solution. The match of information to mental model *is* the solution.

The limitations of intuitive problem-solving

Intuitive problem-solving has proved remarkably successful. After all, it's kept the species going for a few hundred thousand years. Because pattern-matching is more or less unconscious, it's super-sensitive. It picks up subtle cues in a situation, it reads signals in others' behaviour very efficiently and it can spot discrepancies that might be signs of danger. Because pattern-matching is wired directly into our bodies' systems, it triggers action very efficiently. Above all, pattern-matching helps us solve problems quickly. It's fast.

But intuitive problem-solving isn't without its limitations. Here are some of the most important.

Intuitive problem-solving makes us specialists

As we go through life matching mental models to new experiences, we reinforce the mental models that work successfully. The more successful a mental model becomes, the less likely we are to use alternative mental models in similar situations.

As a result, intuitive problem-solving tries to solve the same problem the same way every time. Faced with new information, it likes to 'bolt on': to assimilate new information into an already existing mental model. It's easier to learn butterfly stroke if you can already swim freestyle. A French person can probably learn Italian more easily than Mandarin. 'Bolting on' is the easy mental option. We prefer 'bolt-on' solutions because they need less thinking.

The danger, of course, is that a 'bolt-on' solution may not be the best one. 'Bolting on' may be more efficient than reinvention, but it may not provide the most effective course of action. (Information technology provides many examples of this conundrum.) By extending existing mental models and refining them, we build expertise in specific fields. Our knowledge and skill tend to deepen more readily than they broaden. The field may be huge – the breadth and scope of a whole language, for example – or it may be highly localized, such as the ecology of lichen or pottery techniques in Bhutan.

Specialization is a double-edged sword. It helps us solve problems in our chosen field, but it can limit our thinking when problems fail to sit comfortably within that field. As specialists, we can become more expert but potentially less creative.

Intuitive problem-solving is vulnerable to biases

It's very difficult to catch ourselves making errors when we're practising intuitive problem-solving. All that selective pattern-matching means that we simply don't notice when we miss something, or interpret it inaccurately.

Intuitive problem-solving usually makes reasonable sense of reality, but sometimes it can be wildly wrong. For hundreds of years it was intuitively obvious to most people that the Sun orbited the Earth. (A survey in 2008 suggested that a third of all Americans still believe this.) Many people find it hard to believe that heavy and light objects will fall to the ground at the same rate. Our intuitive judgement is prone to take our perceptions as true, and to forget that they are the result of mental models selecting information from the environment. As a result, intuitive problem-solving is vulnerable to a whole range of biases that can distort our perception and judgement. (We look at some of them in Chapter 10.)

Intuitive problem-solving can generate false solutions

Intuitive problem-solving can sometimes make us see meaning where none exists. The brain hates randomness: if it can use a mental model to find meaningful patterns in chaotic arrangements of information, it will do so. We see images in photographs or clouds; we read significance into the astrology columns in the newspapers; we generate conspiracy theories to account for threats or appalling tragedies.

The fancy name for this capacity to see significance where none exists is *pareidolia*. Some people call it magical thinking because we might explain a problem by identifying a cause that doesn't exist, or by making false correlations between sets of data. We may even resort to blame or superstition in an effort to make sense of the inexplicable. (There's more on blame in Chapter 4.)

Can you see what it is yet?

In an experiment reported in *Science* in 2008, a team from the University of Texas in Austin and Northwestern University in Evanston, Illinois, asked people what patterns they could see in random arrangements of dots or stock market information.

Half the participants had been made to feel a lack of control – either by being given negative feedback unrelated to the way they performed the task or by asking them to remember situations in which they had lost control. These participants tended to see patterns in random information more readily.

The moral of the story is that we're more likely to engage in magical thinking when we feel powerless. When we sense that we lack control in a situation, we can start to see connections between unconnected phenomena and patterns in chaos. We can begin to see meaning where none exists.

Pareidolia can become a serious problem if we feel vulnerable. A gambler on a losing streak, for example, may construct all sorts of illusory patterns to convince himself that he should make the big bet. Workers threatened with redundancy may read all sorts of significance into managerial pronouncements. Anyone feeling exposed or anxious in high-risk, ambiguous or emotionally charged situations – trading on the stock market, perhaps, or declaring war – can succumb to pareidolia.

Intuitive problem-solving can be positively unhelpful, then, if we aren't feeling mentally or emotionally resilient.

Stuckness (and its opposite)

Intuitive problem-solving usually knows what to do. But sometimes it breaks down. And that's when we notice that we've got a problem.

We can define having a problem as:

knowing we want to do something, but not knowing what to do.

This isn't my definition. I've taken it from one of the classic texts on the subject: *Human Problem Solving*, by Allen Newell and Herbert Simon. Newell and Simon put it like this:

"A person is confronted with a problem when he wants something and does not know immediately what series of actions he can perform to get it."

We notice we have a problem when we're *stuck*.

The anatomy of stuckness

Stuckness is a fascinating phenomenon. For example, other animals very rarely get stuck. And very young humans usually avoid being stuck very successfully. Stuckness is a condition that seems to emerge when our capacity to think reaches a certain level of sophistication. Here are some of its more intriguing features.

Stuckness is made up of two elements: our *desire* to do something and our *inability to do it*. Both elements are important, and in thinking about a problem we need to retain sight of both. Our inability to solve a problem drives our search to understand more about the problem; but our desire drives our search to solve it.

There are two kinds of stuckness. We can call them *focused stuckness* and *unfocused stuckness*:

- You experience *focused stuckness* when you can't take your mind off a problem, when it occupies your thinking at the expense of everything else. You're staring at the coffee table where you *know* the car keys should be sitting – and they're not there. You try repeatedly to follow a computer protocol and it refuses to work. You find it impossible to shake off the memory of an offensive customer who upset you earlier in the day. (The problem described by Robert M. Pirsig in Chapter 24 of *Zen and the Art of Motorcycle Maintenance* – from which I quote at the start and end of this book – is a classic example of focused stuckness.)

  Focused stuckness makes us *brood*.

- You experience *unfocused stuckness* when you're overwhelmed by a crowd of problems, when you can't concentrate. You have a dozen demands on your time and you've no idea where to start. You're responsible for completing a project and need to accommodate the actions and demands of a large group of people. You feel you're spending your day 'fire-fighting' rather than getting any real work done.

  Unfocused stuckness makes us *panic*.

Stuckness makes problem-solving conscious. The intuitive problem-solving cycle operates unconsciously. The moment we experience stuckness, we become conscious of our situation.

Stuckness opens up a space in the problem-solving cycle. A gap opens up in our mind between the problem and solution. Problem-solving becomes a two-part process: investigate the problem and generate a solution.

We can fill the problem-solving space with two kinds of thinking. Intuitive problem-solving can still be useful to us, even if we feel it's broken down. Because we're now consciously thinking about the problem, we can reflect on our intuitive responses: we can question them, develop them and guide them. We can start to guide our intuition consciously. And we can now also think about the problem more consciously: using logic, evaluation and analysis. As well as intuitive problem-solving, we can now also start to do rational problem-solving.

Solutions unstick our thinking

Solutions are what we do to escape stuckness. The word 'solve' itself contains the clue to this idea. It comes from the Latin *solvere*, meaning 'to loosen'. To solve a problem is to unknot our thinking about it and create movement: to become unstuck. A *solution* is both the settling of a problem and a fluid created by mixing solids with liquids (*dissolving* them).

A solution, then, is:

  a course of action that unsticks stuckness.

We often talk about 'looking for a solution', 'searching for the answer'. But if a solution to a problem is a course of action, we can't *find* it; we can only *do* it.

The two stages of problem-solving

The aim of problem-solving is to escape from stuckness.

When we're stuck, a space opens up in our thinking: a gap between understanding a problem and generating a solution. In that gap, we can begin to do a new kind of problem-solving. We can begin to think *deliberately*: to test our perceptions and intuitions, to examine the evidence, to look at the problem in different ways and to contemplate alternative solutions.

The first step in unsticking our thinking is to split it into two stages:

Stage 1:   *Identify the problem*
Stage 2:   *Decide what to do*

In Stage 1, we investigate the problem. We gather information about the problem and try to make sense of it. The output of Stage 1 is a representation of the problem. We show the problem to ourselves (we *re*-present it) using language or symbols, a picture or a model. We might name the problem as 'financial' or 'administrative'. We might simplify the problem into an equation: a circuit diagram represents the complex wiring of an electrical system; a map represents the complexity of a landscape; a model represents an aircraft.

In Stage 2, we generate a solution. We examine the information we've gathered and use it to decide what to do. The output of Stage 2 is action. We work with our representation of the problem: we use financial tools to solve financial problems, and administrative systems to solve administrative problems. We can use the circuit diagram to repair the electrical system; we can use the map to find our way out of a forest; we can put the model of the aircraft in a wind-tunnel and observe its aerodynamic behaviour.

Intuitive problem-solving: the magic of reframing

As we've seen, intuitive problem-solving, effective though it is, has some serious limitations. It tends to make us specialists, which can limit our cognitive fluidity. It's vulnerable to biases, which can influence our judgement without us noticing. And it can offer false solutions by generating illusory information.

But intuitive problem-solving has one feature that can unstick our thinking. We can demonstrate this feature using a second visual illusion. (It's called a Rubin vase, after the Danish psychologist Edgar Rubin – see Figure 1.4.)

Figure 1.4 The Rubin vase

Looked at one way, this is a white vase on a black background. Looked at another, it's two heads in profile on a white background. Most people can switch effortlessly between the two images, because the image cunningly matches *two* mental models, and the brain can switch from one to the other.

The Rubin vase demonstrates, in a very simple way, our ability to *reframe*. Faced with new information, intuitive problem-solving can compare it against different mental models and see which fits best. Switching mental models allows us to find the most appropriate thing to do.

In other words, reframing allows us to think about problems *in context*.

Reframing originally evolved as a way of assessing risk: it helped us decide very fast, for example, whether the rustling in the bushes was likely to be a dangerous predator or just the wind at play. And that allowed us to conserve valuable energy.

We reframe whenever we have to decide what to do in complicated or ambiguous situations. Reframing helps us drive, for example: anticipating how that cyclist might shoot out between two lorries, or how that small child might chase its ball into the road. Reframing helps us understand metaphors: if someone tells us to 'pull the door to behind us' when we leave a building, reframing tells us that we're not supposed to wrench the door off its hinges and drag it behind us down the street. Complicated conversations are impossible without the ability to reframe: how else would we be able to adjust our remarks to Richard, knowing that Bharti is behind him listening to every word? (All of these situations would be problematic for anyone diagnosed with a condition on the autistic spectrum. Autistic people often find reframing very difficult.)

Reframing tends to operate instantaneously. We can switch between the two images in the Rubin vase at once; there's no intermediate stage where we're trying to work out rationally how one image differs from another. The suddenness of reframing makes it feel magical. We're baffled; and then, suddenly, the pattern of the solution forms itself in our mind. The moment of intuitive insight often comes with a little emotional explosion: we might cry 'Aha!' or burst out laughing. (Intuitive problem-solving is always closely linked to emotion, as we shall see in Chapter 2.)

Reframing is one of the most powerful of intuitive problem-solving techniques. We'll see how we can develop our ability to reframe to help us look at problems in different ways, and we'll see how at various points throughout this book, especially in Chapter 9.

Rational problem-solving: thinking deliberately

Rational problem-solving operates by deliberate, conscious thought. Three key principles dictate its workings:

1. Understanding the problem and solving the problem are two distinct forms of thinking.
2. Making sense of the problem always means testing our understanding against objective criteria and evidence.
3. Generating a solution always involves building feasibility into the action we propose to take.

Rational problem-solving uses a range of tools and techniques to understand problems and build feasible solutions: measurement, analysis, comparison, logic, evaluation. It also uses models: not mental models, but constructed, objective models that represent the problem we're working on.

Solving problems: two approaches compared

Intuitive problem-solving	*Rational problem-solving*
Purpose: to discover what to do	Purpose: to work out what's true
Recognizes the truth	Works out the truth logically
Pattern-matches	Challenges pattern-matches
Accepts assumptions	Questions assumptions
Trusting: what you see is what there is	Sceptical: what you see is never the whole truth
Finds evidence for hypothesis	Seeks evidence to disprove hypothesis
Seeks similarities	Seeks differences
Combines information into patterns	Analyses information into constituent parts
Spontaneous	Deliberate
Discontinuous	Incremental
Instantaneous	Slow
Polarized: either/or	Discriminating: many possibilities
Discards irrelevant information	Investigates evidence exhaustively
Decisive	Cautious
Acts swiftly	Pauses
The solution explains the problem	The solution removes the problem

The curse of the right answer

Intuitive and rational problem-solving have quite different objectives:

- The aim of intuitive problem-solving is to identify *what to do*.
- The aim of rational problem-solving is to work out *what's true*.

But we often confuse the two objectives. And one of the results of that confusion is something I like to call *the curse of the right answer*.

The idea that a problem must have a correct answer is one of the key features of rational problem-solving. In ancient Greek, the word πρόβλημα ['problema'] meant 'a question posed for a solution'. It particularly referred to a puzzle in logic: a question as to whether a statement is true, to be answered using reasoning.

This idea of a problem as a question that must be answered persists to this day. We solve crosswords and Sudoku in the newspaper; we buy books of problems and join pub quiz teams. Our education system is still dominated by an examination system in which the principal means of succeeding is finding correct answers: a system that can decide our course through life.

Find the right answer and you have won. Fail to find the right answer, and you're a loser.

Of course, very few problems in real life have single, correct answers. Or, to put the point another way: we sometimes confuse two ideas of a solution:

1. a solution as a *conclusion*; and
2. a solution as a *course of action*.

We see this confusion most clearly when we talk about 'fixing' a problem. A 'fix' is a course of action that's also a 'correct' answer: it seems to satisfy both demands of a solution. 'Fix': the very opposite of the idea of a solution as fluid or dynamic. A 'fix' is static, permanent – fixed, indeed. 'I want to fix the problem so it stays fixed', say many of the participants on my problem-solving courses.

A 'fix' puts something right; which means that it must have been wrong to begin with. And so is born the idea that a problem is something 'wrong'. And, by a kind of intuitive association, we see what's wrong as bad. So problems in the real world – unlike the puzzles in the newspaper or the questions on the television quiz show – come to be seen as undesirable things to have, and probably someone's fault. (Notice the link between the two meanings of the word: 'fault' as something wrong, and 'fault' as being responsible for something wrong.) All of which generates a powerful emotional response.

Going ballistic

Interestingly, the '-blem' part of the word 'problem' derives from other words to do with throwing: it's related to the Greek word βάλλειν ['ballein'], meaning 'to throw'. 'Pro-' suggests the idea of 'forward'; so a problem is something 'thrown at us'. And that Greek word 'ballein' is also apparently the root of the word 'ballistic' – which is, of course, what we may go when faced with a problem.

This is the curse of the right answer. It's a curse because it severely limits our abilities as problem-solvers.

If we see a problem as 'bad' or 'wrong', the rational solution must be to put it right; to 'fix' it. We might *remove* what's wrong, or *repair* it. Alternatively, we might look for the *cause* of what went wrong and try to fix that.

Some problems *can* be fixed, of course. If an electric bulb has stopped working, I can replace it. If the chain on my bicycle breaks, I can repair it. If my computer repeatedly shows a mysterious message when I boot up, I may be able to find the piece of software that is causing the problem and remove, repair or replace it.

But not every problem can be fixed. We may not be able to remove what's wrong without removing something of value (how can we destroy a tumour without destroying healthy tissue or organs?). Repairing a fault may cause some other element of the system to fail (the new, highly sensitive fuse box installed in our cellar tripped the moment we turned on the old hob in our kitchen). Many problems have no identifiable causes (many medical problems are of this kind); some have multiple causes (social, political or economic problems often fall into this category).

We need to beware the curse of the right answer. Not all problems can be fixed; not all problems are things that are wrong or bad. Not all solutions are answers; solutions to practical problems are courses of action, which cannot be right or wrong but only successful or unsuccessful. Answers are final; courses of action have consequences.

Rational problem-solving, then, comes to our aid when we're stuck. But it can never entirely replace intuitive problem-solving. And indeed, as we'll see, there is a form of intuition *beyond* rationality that can complement and transcend even the subtle play of reasoning. By combining the best of both approaches, we can solve problems more skilfully – and make wiser decisions.

In brief

Intuitive problem-solving uses mental models to explore the world and decide how to act. Intuitive problem-solving is *discontinuous*. It happens suddenly, not incrementally. In intuitive problem-solving:

- making sense of the problem (by pattern-matching) *always* dictates a solution;
- solving the problem always means *doing something*; and
- solving the problem is also simultaneously a way of understanding the problem better.

Intuitive problem-solving has four main limitations:

1 It's not good at generating alternative solutions.

2 It's vulnerable to biases that can cloud our understanding.

3 It isn't good at noticing when information is missing.

4 We tend to become specialists as intuitive problem-solvers.

When intuitive problem-solving breaks down, we become stuck. **We can define having a problem as knowing we want to do something, but not knowing what to do.**

- Stuckness is made up of two key elements: our *desire* to do or achieve something, and our *inability to do it*.
- There are two kinds of stuckness: focused and unfocused.
- Stuckness makes problem-solving conscious. Stuckness opens up a space in the problem-solving cycle.
- We can fill the problem-solving space with two kinds of thinking.

A solution is a course of action that unsticks our thinking. The first step in unsticking our thinking is to split it into two stages:

- **Stage 1:** **Identify the problem**
- **Stage 2:** **Decide what to do**

Intuitive problem-solving includes contextual thinking, which allows us to view problems in different ways.

Rational problem-solving uses deliberate, step-by-step, conscious thought. In rational problem-solving:

- understanding the problem and solving the problem are two distinct forms of thinking;

- making sense of the problem always means testing our understanding against objective criteria and evidence; and

- generating a solution always involves building feasibility into the action we propose to take.

The principal limitation of rational problem-solving is the **curse of the right answer.**

Chapter

2

Welcome to your brain: nature's problem-solver and how it works (sort of)

Humans are undoubtedly nature's most versatile problem-solvers to date. As we've seen, the key to our success lies in the interplay of two kinds of mental activity:

1. **Intuitive problem-solving** is the work of unconscious pattern-matching: it looks for similarities between problems and puts problems in context to help us decide what to do.
2. **Rational problem-solving** is the work of conscious, deliberate thinking: it uses logic, evidence and evaluation according to objective criteria, rather than association with experience.

And where does this intuitive and rational thinking happen? The obvious answer is: in our brains.

In this chapter we'll take a tour of the brain, exploring the different ways in which it can help us to solve problems – and sometimes get in the way. We'll look at:

- how **emotions** can solve problems for us (or not);
- how problems cause **stress**, how the stress response works and how we can manage it;
- how **reasoning** can open up our thinking to new explanations and arguments;
- how our **multiple intelligences** help us specialize as problem-solvers; and
- how **cognitive fluidity** opens up huge potential in our problem-solving capabilities.

And because all of these different elements operate inside our heads, it makes sense at this point to take …

A quick tour of your brain

Your brain is the most complex system known to man. It weighs about 1.4 kilograms and contains about 100 billion neurons. Each neuron can make contact with thousands of others, using structures called synapses. Your brain makes a million connections between neurons every second, mapping out networks of connections that grow, combine and change as we think and feel. The brain's neural networks are infinitely flexible; and the number of possible neural networks in one brain easily exceeds the number of particles in the known universe.

One way to simplify the workings of this extraordinary organ is to concentrate on three areas:

1. the basal ganglia;
2. the limbic system; and
3. the neocortex.

Each system represents a different stage in our ability to solve problems.

Interestingly, these systems are stacked around each other in the brain: the basal ganglia at the centre, surrounded by the limbic system, with the neocortex folded over the top (see Figure 2.1).

The basal ganglia: helping us do what we know how to do

The basal ganglia are situated at the base of the forebrain. The most intuitive of our intuitive problem-solving happens here.

In particular, the basal ganglia are associated with what the experts call 'procedural memory'. We use procedural memory to perform repeated actions unconsciously: typing or driving a car, singing or playing tennis. By performing the same task many times, we teach our brain to 'pattern in' all the relevant neural systems to work together automatically.

Many problems are interruptions to procedural memory. That feeling of stuckness may arise because something has taken us 'out of procedure'. (We explore this situation more fully in Chapter 4.)

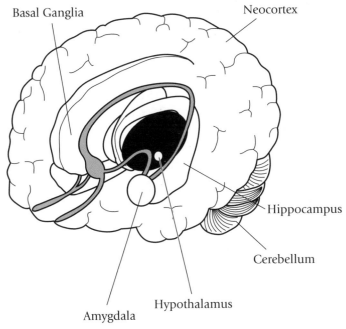

Figure 2.1 The human brain

What to do

Problems that interrupt procedural memory

Think about the last time your procedural memory was interrupted. What was your response?

All sorts of things can disrupt our procedural memory. Imagine trying to teach a child how to tie their shoelaces. Imagine suddenly losing control of the steering while driving, or trying to read a newspaper upside down. In such situations, procedural memory can't operate and we are forced to concentrate consciously on what we're doing: instead of performing like an expert, we're suddenly stumbling about like a beginner (a condition known as 'choking').

Because procedural memory is unconscious, 'choking' can cause strong unconscious responses: anger, frustration or stress.

The limbic system: emotions, memories and stress responses

The limbic system influences intuitive problem-solving by regulating memory and emotion. This area consists of a number of structures, including:

- the **hippocampus** (named for its shape: it's the Latin for 'seahorse'), which is crucial for memory; and

- the **amygdala** (again named for its shape: the Latin for 'almond'), which is closely associated with our emotions (it's been called 'the brain's alarm system').

The term 'limbic' comes from the Latin *limbus*, meaning 'border'. The limbic system sits in the borderland between the conscious and the unconscious. On the one hand, it's a crucial component of intuitive problem-solving: it influences the body's various nervous systems and the release of hormones – all of which governs our behaviour unconsciously. On the other hand, the limbic system is closely wired into the neocortex, where most of our rational problem-solving goes on.

The neocortex: reasoning, planning and communicating

The neocortex sits on and around the rest of the brain, and it's where we do most of our rational problem-solving. It's a sheet of material – no more than two or three millimetres thick – that's responsible for speech, working memory, planning and reasoning. If unfolded, your neocortex would be about the size of a dinner napkin.

Everything we think about with our neocortex has arrived there by way of the limbic system. That's one reason why intuitive and rational problem-solving can only work well if they work *together*.

How our emotions solve problems for us

We saw in Chapter 1 how we solve many problems intuitively, by pattern-matching. We fit new experiences to mental models that tell us what to do. And pattern-matching seems to happen not so much in the neocortex but in the limbic system.

The limbic system acts as a kind of mental receptionist for all external stimuli. It analyses an external stimulus to decide whether it's familiar (through memory) and whether it's friendly or threatening (the basic emotional response). It's the limbic system that tells you whether the shadow in the corner is a ghost or your dressing gown. It's the limbic system that activates the stress response when you start a public speaking engagement, and defuses it after a few minutes as you discover that it's going well. As Daniel Goleman explains in *Emotional Intelligence*:

'When we are in the grip of craving or fury, head-over-heels in love or recoiling in dread, it is the limbic system that has us in its grip.'

The limbic system pattern-matches to a stimulus before sending information to the neorcortex. It can be anything up to half a second before we become consciously aware of what our limbic system has already responded to. And by that time, the amygdala has told us how to react, by generating an emotional response.

Emotions are the limbic system's problem-solving tools. Their function is to make us act. (The word 'emotion' of course includes the word 'motion', and derives from a Latin word meaning 'to remove, expel, to banish from the mind, to shift or to displace'.)

Emotions are simple. According to Paul Ekman, an anthropologist who has studied the expression of emotions around the world, humans exhibit six basic emotions. Each emotion is a mental model that provides a solution for a presented problem:

1. *Anger* causes our heart rate to go up, providing more oxygen to the main muscle groups, and blood flows to our hands to help us grasp a weapon. Anger also triggers the release of adrenaline to give us energy and increased attention.
2. *Fear*, in contrast, sends blood to the legs and feet, to help us run away. In consequence our faces become pale and cold (our 'blood runs cold'). Hormones put us on general alert and fix our attention on the single point where we perceive the threat.

3. *Surprise* opens the eyes to allow us to see more.

4. *Sadness* slows the metabolism and decreases energy, so that we move and do less – perhaps allowing us to stay close to others who will care for us.

5. *Disgust* is principally mediated through the sense of smell (we 'turn up our nose' at something), probably to protect us from poisonous or decayed food.

6. *Happiness* relaxes bodily systems, reduces blood pressure and slows breathing so that we can remain calm. Brain activity inhibits negative emotions and prepares us to work or achieve a goal.

The limbic system can act in two ways. When emotional arousal is low, the limbic system does some contextual thinking, interrogating the pattern-match and comparing it to previous experiences. It then sends information up into the neocortex, which can decide the appropriate response to this specific problem.

If an emotional arousal is strong enough, however, the limbic system adopts a fast-track approach. It cuts off connections with the neocortex, so that information cannot reach the conscious mind. Instead, we act directly on the emotion. We explode with anger, collapse into tears, cry out with surprise, recoil with disgust, scream with fear or burst out laughing. In the words of Daniel Goleman, the limbic system hijacks the neocortex.

When an emotion is solving a problem for us, we act without thinking. If we're highly aroused emotionally, we can't think rationally.

What to do

Is emotion clouding your judgement?

If you think that emotion is preventing you from thinking clearly about a problem, there's only one wise solution: lower the emotional arousal.

Walk away; buy time; discharge the emotion physically by taking exercise, having a good cry or relaxing.

Are you having to deal with another person who is emotionally aroused?

The same principle applies. You will not be able to reason with them. Their brain is being hijacked by their limbic system, and emotion is telling them what to do.

You can either leave them alone, or help them to lower the emotional arousal. Help can be in the form of distracting conversation or activity, telling them to concentrate on their breathing, or assuring them that there is time to calm down. (These are techniques usefully put into practice by the parents of toddlers the world over, to stop tantrums. You can adopt the same techniques, when necessary, with your manager.)

It is never a good idea to fuel the emotional arousal by responding emotionally.

Emotions are part of intuitive problem-solving's repertoire of solutions. They are valid as long as the problem warrants the emotional arousal. But if we respond to a problem using *only* our emotions, we may find that the solution is inappropriate or inadequate.

Intuitive problem-solving, therefore, benefits from some emotional intelligence (EI). According to Daniel Goleman, EI embraces two kinds of awareness:

1. understanding ourselves, our goals, intentions, responses, feelings and behaviours; and
2. understanding others' goals, intentions, responses, feelings and behaviours.

By knowing what arouses our emotions, we can better manage them. By recognizing emotional responses in others, we can help them manage their emotions. By understanding how emotions work, we can deal with them more calmly and productively.

Problems and stress

Problems can cause stress. And we also know that stress is bad for our well-being. Understanding stress is critically important if we want to become better problem-solvers – and if we want to remain healthy.

Stress is one of the inevitable consequences of being stuck. If we want to do something, but we don't know what to do, we feel vulnerable in a situation of potential danger. That's stress. The environmental nasties – the things we call problems – are usually called *stressors*, and the reactions they stimulate – biological and psychological – are referred to as *the stress response*.

Stress is the interaction of stressors and stress response. The same stressor can cause wildly different responses in different people; and the same level of response can be triggered by very different stressors. The collapsed omelette that causes one cook to explode in frustration may cause barely a shrug in another. A fault on a computer may rouse one user to intense interest and cause considerable anxiety in another. An encounter with poor road manners can trigger laughter in some drivers but road rage in others.

The stress response is another of nature's intuitive problem-solving mechanisms. In essence, it's a two-track process. Here's how it works.

Fight or flight

As with emotions, the stress response is born in the limbic system. It operates unconsciously; our chances of survival are better if we act without thinking.

If the limbic system identifies a stressor, it activates the sympathetic nervous system (SNS). The normal function of the SNS is to maintain our bodies in a state of dynamic equilibrium called homeostasis, by regulating temperature, blood sugar levels, digestive acids and so on. When faced with a stressor, the system releases adrenaline and noradrenaline; these two hormones trigger the fight-or-flight response.

Fight or flight seeks to solve a problem by switching priorities: from long-term homeostasis to short-term survival. It's this switching of priorities that causes the familiar symptoms of the response:

- Fuel is transported rapidly through the blood system to the brain. (Pulse and blood pressure rise.)
- Blood is taken from the smaller muscle groups at our extremities to the larger muscle groups. (We get cold feet – literally.)
- Systems regulating long-term well-being (growth, digestion, sex) are sacrificed in favour of the systems that will help you fight or fly. (We lose appetite and our ability to salivate, we get 'butterflies in the stomach' and a dry mouth. Libido collapses.)
- The pupils dilate (so that we can see more) and we get 'tunnel vision'.
- Our palms and feet become sweaty to improve our grip.
- Alertness and reaction times are improved (we become 'jumpy').
- Sphincters at each end of the digestive system relax: we become nauseous and may feel the need to defecate or urinate, partly to lose weight and partly, perhaps, to make us less attractive to a predator.

As a result, fight or flight is a double-edged problem-solving sword. It's vital if we're facing an imminent threat to our physical safety, but it's not so helpful if the problem is more complicated, subtle or long-lasting. As a response to the stressors of modern life, it can be wildly inappropriate. We may want to decapitate our manager when they make unreasonable demands, or rush screaming from a meeting when an argument gets heated, but those options are not (usually) available.

Can stress help us to solve problems?

Yes, it can.

For a start, it makes us concentrate. Adrenaline and noradrenaline help us to focus on the problem at hand. This single-mindedness comes at a cost, however: we become unable to think flexibly. As with intense emotional arousal, heightened stress cuts the neural pathways between the limbic system and the neocortex, making us less capable of rational thought and subtle discrimination.

Fight or flight also seems to include a reward for enduring the stress. The response includes the release of endorphins: chemicals not unlike morphine or heroin. Endorphins relax us; at high levels, they can lower our perception of pain. They also seem to be partly responsible for our feelings of satisfaction or elation when we've endured a stressful experience. Endorphins may be implicated in 'runners' high', the euphoria some athletes experience after strenuous exercise.

These benefits, however, also come at a cost. The same endorphins that suppress pain and give us 'natural highs' can suppress the activity of natural killer cells and increase the risk of developing tumours.

The key seems to be to keep stress levels at an intermediate level: too much stress – or too little – and performance suffers. Indeed, if the stress response is brief, mild and – crucially – controllable it can become positively enjoyable. This kind of positive stress has been called *eustress*. The term's not often used, but we've all experienced eustress in the thrill of a rollercoaster ride or a horror movie. We can induce eustress by winning a race, getting a promotion – or by solving a really tough problem.

The really good news is that the fight-or-flight response is short-lived. It kicks in within 30 seconds of a stressor being identified, and usually subsides within about an hour.

If the stressor *doesn't* go away, however – or if we face a series of short-term stressors over a period of time – we may find ourselves succumbing to a second stress response. And it's far more serious than the first.

Long-term stress and its dangers

This second response is activated by the hypothalamus–pituitary–adrenal system (the HPA axis, as it's sometimes known). A complicated sequence of electrical and chemical messages in this system releases a cocktail of substances, among the most important of which is cortisol.

Cortisol is a substance not unlike the steroids doctors use to treat inflammation and allergies. Its function is to convert energy reserves into forms the body can use immediately.

Normally, levels of cortisol rise and fall rhythmically during the day, in line with our demand for energy.

Persistently high levels of cortisol can cause serious harm. Long-term disruption of cortisol's natural cycle, for example, can lead to insomnia, burnout or chronic fatigue – not to mention a range of mood disorders including depression, anxiety and addiction. Over time, cortisol can suppress the immune system, making us more susceptible to infection. By mobilizing energy reserves, cortisol can release fatty acids into the bloodstream, increasing the risk of clogged arteries and heart disease. Other chemical reactions can contribute to a whole range of mood disorders, including depression, anxiety and alcoholism.

What makes long-term stress even more serious is the very fact that it is long-lasting. Unlike the fight-or-flight response, which can subside within an hour, the long-term stress response can persist for days, or even weeks.

And it gets worse

Stress may bring some benefits, but overall it does a lot more harm than good.

The two stress responses operate in a complicated relationship. Exposing ourselves to multiple small stressors can activate the longer, slower response. Continual small-scale problem-solving ('fire-fighting') can result in long-term stress.

And the stress responses can't be suppressed – only discharged. Pretending that we're not suffering stress, or trying to struggle on and ignore the symptoms of long-term stress, simply fuels the response. The only way to reduce stress is to reduce the levels of stress-inducing substances.

What to do

Are you suffering from long-term stress?

Check out these symptoms (the list is not exhaustive). They often accumulate until you are forced to take notice of them. You may notice the behavioural symptoms first; but they can show themselves *after* stress has been going on for some time.

▶

Don't rationalize the symptoms away. If you're not sure, ask your GP.

Behavioural signs

- Becoming a workaholic: no time to relax
- Poor time management or poor standards of work
- Absenteeism
- Social withdrawal and relationship problems
- Insomnia or waking tired

Psychological signs

- Inability to concentrate or make simple decisions
- Memory lapses
- Depression and anxiety

Emotional signs

- Tearfulness and irritability
- Mood swings: sudden outbursts of anger or frustration
- Feeling out of control
- Lack of motivation
- Lack of confidence or self-esteem

Physical signs

- Aches and pains, muscle tension, grinding teeth
- Frequent colds or infections
- Constipation, diarrhoea, irritable bowel syndrome (IBS)
- Weight loss or gain
- Indigestion, heartburn, ulcers, nausea
- Dizziness, palpitations
- Panic attacks
- Physical tiredness
- Menstrual changes, loss of libido, sexual problems
- Heart problems, high blood pressure

What can stress teach us?

What's the moral of all this for us, as problem-solvers?

Problems cause stress. Stress is the result of an interaction between a stressor and a stress response. The interaction varies greatly between individuals, but it always works on two levels: short-term and long-term.

Short-term stress can help us solve problems. It increases concentration and includes a built-in reward mechanism to make us feel good when we've solved the problem.

Long-term stress, in contrast, is almost entirely harmful. It can increase the risk of infection, heart disease, skin rashes, high blood pressure, migraine, asthma, gastrointestinal disease, depression, anxiety, addiction and some cancers. It can even affect the ageing process.

The stress response limits our ability to think fluidly. It shuts down contextual thinking, inhibits rational thinking and promotes action. We can never, therefore, successfully suppress a stress response; we can only successfully discharge it.

How to manage your stress responses

If we want to develop our problem-solving abilities, we need to be able to manage our stress responses.

We can manage stress in many ways. We could seek to discharge the stress response physically; we could manage our diet and examine our environment for sources of unnecessary stress; and we could manage our own behaviour to make us more tolerant of stress. Finally, we could seek to deal with the stressor itself: we could start to develop our problem-solving skills.

Exercise and breathing

The stress response is physical. It makes sense, therefore, to find ways of discharging the response physically.

The stress response is designed to make us respond to problems with vigorous action; but most of us face stressors while sitting at desks or at the wheels of our cars. Regular exercise helps to dispel stress hormones and other neurochemicals, and keeps them at healthy levels. Exercise also helps us sleep better, almost certainly helps us think better and is a potent antidepressant.

What to do

7:11 breathing

One of the first things to suffer when we get stressed is our breathing. In particular, we start breathing *in* more than we breathe out. Result: we start to asphyxiate. This exercise is designed to reverse the behaviour. The aim is to breathe *out* more than you breathe *in*. It will automatically calm you and reduce your stress level. Guaranteed!

1 Assume a comfortable position if possible and close your eyes if you wish.

2 Take a slow breath in to the count of 7.

3 Hold for a few seconds.

4 Release your breath out slowly to the count of 11.

5 Hold for a few seconds.

Repeat as necessary until you feel yourself calm down.

Any activity that involves deep breathing is likely to be effective in reducing stress: singing, cycling, swimming ... Meditation, too, starts with an emphasis on effective breathing. Find what works for you.

Food, drink and other substances

Diet can be a surprisingly important factor in making us vulnerable to stress. If you want to reduce your predisposition to stress, you could consider moderating your intake of these kinds of foods:

- sugar-high foods;
- foods high in salt;
- caffeine;

- foods deficient in Vitamin C and the Vitamin B complex;
- alcohol;
- nicotine.

Removing environmental stressors

Many environmental stressors are avoidable. If you have a headache because you've been reading with poor light, move to another room where the lighting is better. Manage noise levels and think about the design of the chairs you use regularly. Changing your surroundings can mean turning on lights, turning off loud music, raising or lowering your computer chair.

Public spaces can be particularly stressful. Make a careful survey of the places where you spend a good deal of your time. Check your surroundings carefully for potential situational stressors.

Looking after yourself

It's critically important to stop problems overwhelming you. All problems change if we change our response to them. Look after yourself and you'll be able to deal with problems far more effectively:

- **Take breaks.** Take a lunch break and don't talk about work. Take a walk instead of a coffee break. Use weekends to relax, and don't schedule so many leisure events that Monday morning will seem like a relief. Take regular holidays, long weekends or mental-health days at intervals that you have learned are right for you.
- **Create predictability** in your work and home life. Structure and routine in your life can't prevent every surprise, but they can provide the security we all need to be able to deal with the unexpected. Plan ahead.
- **Share problems with others.** Getting someone else's perspective on a problem can help you gain perspective and reduce stress. It can also be helpful for the other person to know that you're facing a problem, so that they can understand your situation and help you more effectively.

- **Learn to say 'no'.** Find your own limits and exercise your skill in keeping to them. You're not much use to others if you're not looking after yourself. You may benefit from developing your time management skills; learn to delegate.

Reasoning: the work of deliberate thought

With reasoning, it seems, we finally emerge from the dark recesses of the limbic system to the higher reaches of the neo-cortex. It's here, in the (literally) highest parts of the brain, that we do the deliberate, conscious work of rational problem-solving.

We saw in Chapter 1 that three key principles dictate the workings of rational problem-solving:

1. Understanding the problem and solving the problem are two distinct forms of thinking.
2. Making sense of the problem always means testing our understanding against objective criteria and evidence.
3. Generating a solution always involves building feasibility into the action we propose to take.

And we do all of this consciously, deliberately and – compared to the lightning responses of intuition, emotion or stress – relatively slowly.

What to do

A crash course in reasoning

To become more competent at rational thinking, follow these simple guidelines.

Reasoning is purposeful:

- Define the problem you're trying to solve as clearly as you can.
- Distinguish the problem from similar or related problems.
- Review your problem definition regularly.

Reasoning always starts from a point of view, a position or an assumption:

- Identify your point of view.
- Identify the assumptions lying behind your point of view and justify them.
- Ask how your assumptions are influencing your definition of the problem.
- Seek other points of view and identify their strengths as well as weaknesses.

Reasoning looks for different views of the problem:

- Express the problem in several ways to clarify its meaning and scope.
- Break the problem into sub-problems.
- Ask whether the problem is a question of truth or action.
- Ask whether you need to use different kinds of reasoning for different parts of the problem.

Reasoning is expressed by, and works with, ideas:

- Identify the key ideas that inform your understanding of the problem.
- Express all key ideas as sentences. Headings or names are not concepts and cannot be assembled into arguments.
- Look for the assumptions underlying your ideas and challenge them.
- Consider alternative ideas – especially ideas that contradict your key ideas.

Reasoning assembles ideas into arguments leading to conclusions:

- Identify the idea that is your conclusion, and the ideas that act as reasons to support or lead to the conclusion.
- Ask how the reasons connect to the conclusion.

Reasoning is based on evidence:

- Ask how the data and information you're using acts as evidence for your ideas.
- Search for evidence to disprove your ideas.

▶

Reasoning has consequences:

- Trace the implications of your conclusion.
- Ask how your conclusion implies a course of action.
- Identify the consequences of your chosen course of action.

We usually think of rationality as being separate from intuition and emotion. We're fascinated with characters who can rationalize without being 'infected' by feeling: think of Sherlock Holmes, Mr Spock, or Stanley Kubrick's famous computer Hal (in *2001: A Space Odyssey*).

In truth, of course, reason and intuition are complementary. Our minds can reason only with material we observe, and most of our perception is intuitive. Rationality in the real world constantly cycles between theory and observation, each continually modifying the other. The very act of forming a hypothesis involves recognizing a pattern or a trend: and recognizing patterns is, in essence, intuitive. If we notice that people are falling ill more frequently in one region than in neighbouring regions, it's not logic but intuition that connects the observations into a pattern and tells us something's not right.

Rationality, then, can never operate entirely without intuition. Just as the different parts of the brain operate together, in networks of staggeringly complexity, so we might say that rational problem-solving works best when it's linked to intuition.

And we might say that our ability to combine rationality and intuition to solve problems is a measure of our intelligence.

Intelligence or intelligences?

Intelligence is a tricky concept to pin down. We associate it with quick reasoning: to be labelled 'slow', all too often, is to be regarded as unintelligent. Yet rapid reasoning often makes mistakes. We might confuse intelligence with having lots of knowledge (a confusion encouraged by numerous quiz shows on television); but it's obvious that knowing lots of facts hardly makes someone intelligent. Intelligence quotient (or IQ) is probably the most familiar marker of intelligence; yet IQ has its critics. IQ arguably measures only the more rational aspects of intelligence: our powers of logical deduction, in particular.

Some scientists argue that the mind is made up of multiple intelligences. Howard Gardner, for example, claims to be able to identify eight different types of intelligence (see Figure 2.2). Six relate to our environment: visual, linguistic, logical and mathematical, bodily and kinaesthetic, musical and naturalistic. Gardner completes his list with two types of personal intelligence: interpersonal, which helps us deal with others; and intrapersonal, which helps us examine our own thinking and behaviour.

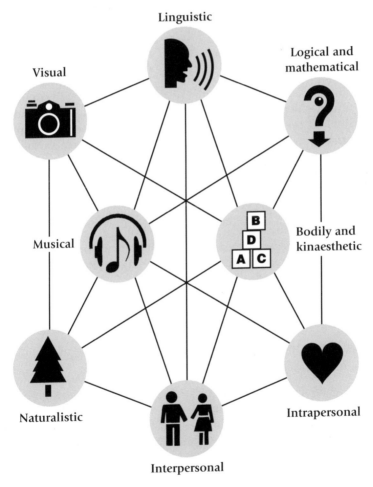

Figure 2.2 Gardner's eight types of intelligence

Gardner defines intelligence in terms of problem-solving. In his book *Frames of Mind*, he writes that, as he sees it, intelligence must be a competence: it 'must entail a set of skills of problem solving – enabling the individual to resolve genuine problems or difficulties that he or she encounters'. Intelligence, he suggests, is not just a way of dealing with problems we encounter, it 'must also entail the potential for *finding* or *creating* problems – and thereby laying the groundwork for the acquisition of new knowledge' (my emphasis).

All of Gardner's intelligences are functional: they all help us *do* things rather than simply *knowing* things. Visual intelligence tells us how to move, linguistic intelligence how to speak, interpersonal intelligence how to behave with others and so on. The theory of multiple intelligences links the brain intimately to the body and reminds us that a solution isn't merely an answer to a question – it's something we *do*.

Gardner points out that his multiple intelligences constantly interact. We can build connections between them to help us solve ever more complex problems. And this idea, too, makes sense. How could musical intelligence operate without invoking bodily and kinaesthetic intelligence to help us sing, dance or play an instrument? How could our linguistic intelligence reach its potential without an interpersonal intelligence to help us understand the impact of our words on others?

And it's because our various intelligences can interact that we can solve problems in so many different ways. Another name for it is 'cognitive fluidity'.

Cognitive fluidity: your mind is (like) a cathedral

Cognitive fluidity is our ability to combine different kinds of intelligence to create new ideas.

Imagine that your mind is like a cathedral. (This idea is based on a model devised by Stephen Mithen in his book, *The Prehistory of the Mind*. I've added one or two elements and adapted his brilliant image for my own purposes.)

This cathedral, like most great cathedrals, has grown up over time; in this case, evolutionary time:

- Underlying the whole edifice is an underground complex: we could call it the 'crypt'. This is where our intuitive problem-solving goes on, matching information to mental models unconsciously.
- Above the crypt is the central 'nave' of the cathedral, where we do generalized reasoning.
- Around the 'nave' are groups of 'chapels', each devoted to a specialized intelligence. We might envisage eight, corresponding to Howard Gardner's multiple intelligences. And we might envisage more and more 'chapels' attaching themselves to the cathedral as we acquire new specialized intelligences.

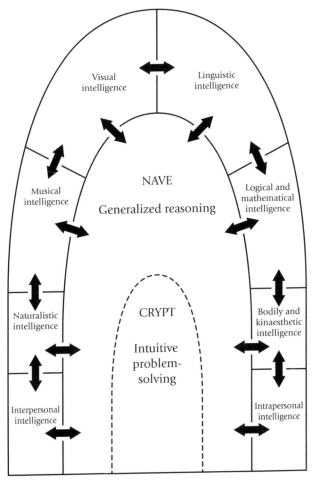

Figure 2.3 The cathedral of the mind

Each of these areas of the cathedral is an area of the mind. Each is distinct, but all are connected: we can imagine doors and windows linking the 'chapels' to the 'nave', as well as stairways leading down from all parts of the building into the 'crypt'.

Our thoughts, like pilgrims, can wander at will around the cathedral, taking ideas and information from one 'chapel' into another, enriching material in different 'chapels' with the general reasoning powers of the 'nave', descending into the 'crypt' and bringing its insights up into the main building.

This is cognitive fluidity. Our multiple intelligences allow us to specialize; cognitive fluidity is the source of our ability to innovate. By combining different intelligences, we can create new solutions to old problems and identify entirely new problems to solve.

Indeed, cognitive fluidity is the source of that most powerful problem-solving tool: imagination.

Chapels, cubicles and silos

Humans are mental specialists – it's an inevitable consequence of intuitive problem-solving. As we saw in Chapter 1, the natural tendency of pattern-matching is to grow expertise in specific fields of experience and knowledge. We think, learn and operate in discrete 'chapels' of knowledge and skill, developing our abilities in greater detail and depth.

Our organizations reflect this specializing tendency. We define ourselves in terms of functional specialisms. We become 'cubicle workers'. The 'chapels' of Stephen Mithen's mental cathedral have become the 'silos' of the modern corporation. And breaking down the walls between them can be difficult.

Yet many problems demand 'cross-cubicle' thinking: a patient being treated by a group of medical specialists; a product-development team innovating a new product or service; a film production using the skills of actors, writers, musicians and a range of technical experts. Social and political problems demand cognitive fluidity, too. Our success as a species is built on cognitive fluidity.

How can we break down the walls in the cathedrals of our minds? What's the secret of cognitive fluidity?

I talk, therefore I solve problems

The answer is language. Language allows us to think about things *in terms of other things*. It helps us to think in new ways, about new things. With language, we can transform our ideas into new ideas. How? In three ways.

First, language allows us to articulate our *intuitions*. We can bring our hunches and insights into the light of consciousness, to reflect on them, challenge them, work with them and – sometimes – act on them.

Second, language allows us to *reason*. By reasoning we can make sense of the world more objectively than by relying simply on intuition and experience. We can work out what *evidence* means, and sort evidence into meaningful *categories*. Language allows us to construct *ideas* with which we can generalize from evidence. And with language we can assemble our ideas into *explanations*, by which we can evaluate the significance of what we know, and *arguments*, which give us objective reasons for choosing solutions.

But language, finally, is also the key to cognitive fluidity. With language, we can create *associations* between things, in terms of *closeness*, *opposition* or *similarity*. Associative thinking opens up the possibility of thinking about things in terms of other things: by means of *simile*, *analogy* and *metaphor*. Language – to speak metaphorically – is the power that blows holes in the walls of our mental cathedrals, allowing us to combine intelligences in pursuit of new ideas and innovations. All of these faculties put us in touch with the wellsprings of intuitive problem-solving and take it to a new level, in which we can exercise our *imagination* to visualize past events, future scenarios and alternative realities. (We'll explore these powers in more detail in Chapter 9.)

Language, then, allows us to combine the strengths of intuitive and rational problem-solving. And it does one thing more. Language allows us to *share* our thinking – to offer our thinking for others to inspect; and to take the thinking of other people and develop it. Language is the key to collaboration. (And we'll investigate the challenges of collaboration in Chapter 11.)

In brief

The human brain contains three main systems that help us to solve problems in different ways:

1 the basal ganglia;

2 the limbic system; and

3 the neocortex.

The basal ganglia are associated with procedural memory. The limbic system mediates emotional and stress responses. The neocortex is the home of rationality – conscious, deliberate thinking.

- **Procedural memory** combines bottom-up and top-down processing to help us solve routine and familiar problems by 'patterning in' complex actions.

- **Emotions** trigger responses to situations that threaten us or promise some advantage – responses that we can sometimes moderate using rational thought.

- The **stress responses**, both short-term and long-term, can help us perform better as problem-solvers but can also do us serious harm.

- **Reasoning** helps us construct arguments and reach conclusions.

- Our **multiple intelligences** serve us well as problem-solving specialists.

- **Cognitive fluidity** gives us the imagination to look at problems in new ways and combine intelligences to generate innovative solutions.

And how do we navigate all these different levels and types of faculty? By means of language.

Chapter

3

What's your style?: your problem-solving profile and what it means

Problem-solving is all about liberating ourselves from stuckness. You know you have a problem when you want to do something but you don't know what to do. As we've seen in Chapter 1, we have an astonishing array of mental tools and techniques to unstick our thinking. No other animal on earth is such a versatile problem-solver.

Becoming a better problem-solver, then, means becoming even more versatile. All of us favour some forms of thinking over others. We're as much creatures of habit as of creativity. We develop the thinking styles we find successful, and allow the less successful styles to wither. Becoming more versatile means exploiting the styles of thinking we're good at and growing those styles we've used less.

A good place to start is to examine what we already do well. Understanding our preferred problem-solving style is useful in all sorts of ways. It will help us to see why we approach problems in the way we do. But it will also help us to see where we can develop new thinking skills.

This chapter will help you identify the problem-solving styles that work well for you and where your strengths lie. You'll also begin to see where you can grow new skills, to help you solve problems in new ways.

How to assess your preferred problem-solving styles

On the next page you'll find four sets of problem-solving behaviours. Mark as many of the behaviours as you think apply to you. You can mark as many or as few behaviours as you wish. When you've completed the questionnaire, we'll explore what your answers might mean. Try not to turn to the following pages before completing the questionnaire.

This isn't a personality test. It's certainly not in any way scientific. We're looking at preferred behaviours: the things you're most comfortable doing. We can generalize from those behaviours to a set of preferred thinking styles, but these are not in any way intended to indicate what kind of person you are. Thinking styles, like other styles, are behaviours we can choose to adopt.

It's up to you to decide how accurate or revealing the questionnaire is about your preferred thinking styles. The aim is *not* to label or categorize you; the very last thing we should do is judge ourselves as being a type of thinker – or a type of person. The aim here is to identify where you might like to develop your abilities and become a more versatile problem-solver.

OK. Now mark the behaviours you think most obviously describe the way you like to solve problems. Take your time.

Circle all the phrases in each box that best describe your approach to dealing with problems.

1	2
Investigates thoroughly before deciding Works precisely and slowly Looks for causes of problems Prepares and studies in advance Relies on and uses facts to back arguments Asks: 'What ...?' and 'Why ...?' Is numerate Organizes information carefully Knows how to access appropriate databases for relevant facts Looks for differences and distinctions Applies rules to understand information Prefers a lot of detail on which to base decisions	Likes control Likes to make firm decisions Dislikes inaction Prefers maximum freedom to manage oneself and others Applies clear protocols to implement a solution Low tolerance for feelings, attitudes and advice of others Technically proficient Seeks a permanent fix Good at finding faults Asks 'How ...?' Is focused Does not like to waste time

3	4
Seeks unknown territory and new ideas Self-motivated, restless Trusts the spontaneous insight Interested in analogies and resemblances Insatiably curious Seeks out ambiguity and uncertainty Asks: 'What else ...?' and 'What if ...?' Looks for the unanswered questions Enjoys breaking rules Enjoys working at the edge of competence or improvising Likes to take risks Easily bored: finds it hard to follow through or finish	Thinks in pictures Seeks patterns in information Asks: 'Why not ...?' Regards failure as an interesting learning opportunity Tends to dream Thinks about the 'big picture' Seeks inspiration Cultivates 'style' Thrives on feedback Looks for the simplest, most elegant solution Likes selling solutions Capable of judging self-generated ideas objectively

Count up the number of behaviours you have marked in each column and transfer the number onto the grid below.

1: Analyst	2: Engineer
My score:	My score:
3: Explorer	4: Designer
My score:	My score:

Now mark your scores on the target (see Figure 3.1). Mark the lowest scores nearest the centre of the target on each axis. I've added the numbers 6 and 12 on each axis to help you position your scores. Join the dots to create a four-sided shape, like the shape on Figure 3.4. Colour the shape, in whatever way you like. Go ahead, make your shape bold and interesting.

How the style profile works

Your problem-solving profile is based on two axes.

The two stages of problem-solving

The horizontal axis represents the problem-solving process. The left-hand side of the axis represents Stage 1: identifying and describing problems. The right-hand side of the axis represents Stage 2: generating solutions.

Two thinking styles relate to each of these stages (see Figure 3.2):

- Analyst and Explorer are the two styles of Stage 1 problem-solving: defining or describing problems.
- Engineer and Designer are the two styles of Stage 2 problem-solving: generating solutions.

Higher scores on the left side of the profile indicate that you prefer the investigative side of problem-solving to the implementation side. Others might see you as overly cautious, indecisive or unwilling to commit to action.

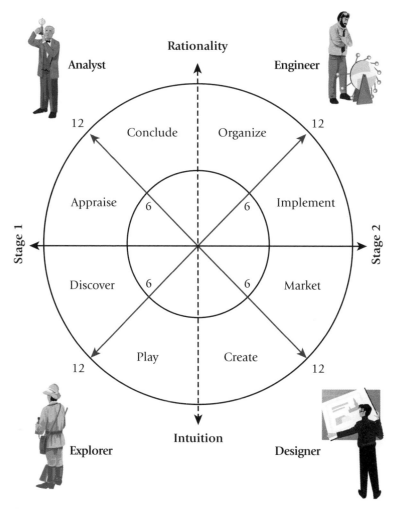

Figure 3.1 The target

Higher scores on the right of the profile might indicate that you prefer to implement rather than investigate. Others might see you as impetuous or impatient, taking action first and asking questions later.

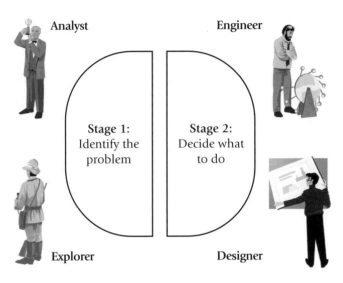

Figure 3.2 Thinking styles linked to stages

Rationality and intuition

The vertical axis on Figure 3.1 represents the way you prefer to look at a problem situation (see Figure 3.3). At the top is rationality; at the bottom is intuition:

- At the top of the axis, you prefer to act rationally *on* your environment. You see reality as something to be encountered, explained and exploited. You are interested in how things are and how you want them to be. A gap in a problem is between what is and what *should* be.

  Analyst and Engineer are the problem-solving styles relating to this view.

- At the bottom end of the axis, you prefer to act intuitively *with* your environment. You see reality as something to be played with, and moulded. You're interested in how things might be, and how you could reveal their potential. A gap in a problem is between what is and what *could* be.

  Explorer and Designer are the problem-solving styles relating to this view.

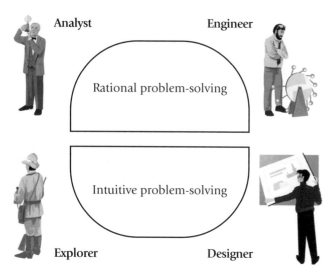

Figure 3.3 The four styles

All problem-solving, of course, moves between all four styles. But many of us will prefer some aspects of problem-solving over others. Your scores suggest the styles that you're most comfortable with.

Let's look at each style in turn, and understand a little more about each.

The Explorer style [Stage 1: intuition]

Explorer is an investigative style. The essence of this style is searching (and researching). Explorer's main assumption is that there is always more to find out.

The two key activities in Explorer are:

1. discovering;
2. playing.

Unlike the Analyst style, exploring is not about working out the truth but about discovering more. You have to know what's around the next corner, beyond the next hilltop. You follow your nose (this is an intuitive style, after all). The Explorer style is curious: you're constantly looking for new information and new ways of thinking about information. You like nothing better than the unexpected, the unconventional and the frankly unacceptable. You take what you've discovered and improvise with it. Forget formulae and accurate calculation; you love playing around, seeing what you can do with what you've discovered. You are always asking 'What else?', and 'What if ...?'. The Explorer style loves challenging assumptions and reversing norms. You thrive on metaphors and resemblances.

Like Engineer, Explorer is risk-friendly. You're easily bored; you are far more inclined to play than create a feasible solution.

What to do

Developing your Explorer style: questions to ask

- Where else can you look for ideas?
- How can you change your viewpoint?
- Where is opportunity knocking?
- What resources are in front of you?
- What ideas from history can help?
- Where can you ask: 'What if ...?'
- What information may be lurking below the surface?
- Where does this information fit into a bigger picture?
- How can you change direction?
- How could you explore differently?
- Where haven't you looked?
- What hunches have you got?

The Analyst style [Stage 1: rational]

 Analyst, like Explorer, is an investigative style. The essence of this style is the desire to make sense of information and situations. Analyst's main assumption is that understanding comes from applying reason to what we know.

The two key activities in Analyst mode are:

1. appraising;
2. concluding.

Analyst is rational. In Analyst mode you gather evidence, organize information and interpret according to formulae, rules or principles. You are good at spotting mistakes and faulty reasoning. In Analyst mode you probably prefer to work alone (although many researchers enjoy working in a team). You like nothing more than asking the Explorer style to find more data: the more, the better. You study the data, and restudy them, searching for the clues that will reveal the hidden truth.

This is a slow-paced style. Decision-making is difficult; you crave information that is complete, and research that is thorough. This is the most risk-averse of the problem-solving styles. People working in Engineer style may be urging you to sign off your results; you might see them as impatient and headstrong.

What to do

Developing your Analyst style: questions to ask

- How can you organize this information?
- Can you break this information down into smaller pieces?
- What's the method?
- Is there a trend?
- What could you eliminate?

►

- What's the real problem?
- What new rules could you use to organize this information?
- Can you test the idea?
- What variables can you alter?
- How do things fit together?
- Are there other categories?
- What can you measure?

The Engineer style [Stage 2: rational]

Engineer is an implementing style. The aim of the Engineer style is creating a solution that works.

Engineer's two key activities are:

1. organizing;
2. implementing.

Engineer, like Analyst, is a rational style. It applies systems, protocols and routines to make things happen. In Engineer style you're interested in how a solution works – and how to make it work better. Think of the word 'engineer' as a verb: to apply technical knowledge to practical problems (the kind of work done by a mechanical engineer or a civil engineer); and to bring about a solution through contrivance, skilful or artful (as in 'she engineered a good result'). Engineer manipulates conditions and resources to bring about the required solution; this style is also interested in managing others to get results.

Unlike Analyst, Engineer tends to be fast-paced. Where Analyst craves accuracy, Engineer craves a workable solution. In your pursuit of a practical solution, you'll do whatever is necessary: organizing resources, people and time to achieve the goal. Engineer is more tolerant of risk than Analyst – although you will always want to test your solution. In Engineer mode, information is only useful if it helps you construct your solution.

What to do

Developing your Engineer style: questions to ask

- Why won't the solution work?
- What's good about this solution?
- How does the solution fit into existing systems?
- Can you make the solution more effective or efficient?
- Can you implement the solution more effectively or efficiently?
- What will be the consequences of implementing this solution?
- Is the solution legally sound?
- Who do you need to help you implement the solution?
- Where will you find the resources to implement this solution?
- How will you measure the solution's success?
- How could you improve the solution?
- Where's the risk?

The Designer style [Stage 2: intuitive]

 The Designer, like Explorer, is an implementing style. The essence of the Designer style is creating a solution that is neat, elegant or beautiful – something that others will find attractive and admirable.

The two key activities in Designer mode are:

1. creating;
2. marketing.

Designer is an intuitive style. Rather than seeing how a solution works, it's interested in how it fits together. Designer's aim is to find a solution that's neat, elegant, beautiful. Designer delights in the process of creating a solution. Designer likes nothing better than to make complexity simple; you are looking for the pattern that will please the eye or the heart, even if the solution is impractical or ineffective (but, you will say, in good design, 'form follows function').

Designer thinks in pictures. You're forever doodling. You are especially keen on the 'big picture', perhaps at the expense of detail, although you may quote Mies van der Rohe, the great architect, who said that 'God is in the detail'. (You may well be rather fond of quoting.) You are drawn to an ideal vision of the future that may be unattainable: both the Analyst and the Engineer modes may need to rein in their imagination. You identify with your ideas, and love selling them to others. You welcome feedback, as long as it is fulsome praise. Criticism may not go down well.

Designer may well also want others to know about its creations. As you shift towards Engineer mode, you look for opportunities to market your creations; indeed, your main focus may be on creating an audience. Designer thrives on attention and praise.

What to do

Developing your Designer style: questions to ask

- What's the neatest solution you can think of?
- Can you rearrange things?
- What can you substitute?
- What does this solution remind you of?
- How would the solution look reversed: inside out, back to front, inside out?
- How would a magician do it?
- What would a six-year-old child see in this solution?
- What rules can you break?
- How can you exaggerate the solution?
- If you were the solution, how would you feel?
- How will others judge the solution?
- How can you defend the solution?

Understanding your own problem-solving profile

Let me repeat this important point: this profile is not a personality test. It does not show, in any way, what kind of person you are. This profile shows where your strengths are likely to be when you're solving problems.

It's important to emphasize, too, that the way you scored yourself is not definitive. You might score differently on a different day, or in different circumstances. You might use your Explorer skills more frequently when managing people, for example, and your Analyst skills more when studying or managing a budget at work. You might use your Engineer skills more when leading a project, and your Designer skills when writing a proposal.

The profile may show, however, which skills you are most comfortable using.

Becoming a more versatile problem-solver

As well as helping us understand where we already work well as problem-solvers, this profile can show us hints about how we can develop our skills. The aim of the exercise, after all, is to become more versatile – so that we can tackle almost any problem!

Which is your most preferred style? (And your least?)

Let's begin with individual styles. Each style brings its own particular strengths to problem-solving. A high score in one style suggests that you are something of an expert in that set of skills; similar scores in more than one style suggests that you are already a versatile problem-solver.

What to do

Examining your problem-solving profile: initial questions
Look at the profile you've drawn for yourself.

- Do you clearly excel in one style?
- Or are you equally proficient in more than one style?
- Is there one style that is definitely low in your own estimate of your abilities?

Now look at your *lowest-scoring* style. You may be able to find some very good reasons why you scored low, but the key question is: how could you develop that style to increase your versatility as a problem-solver?

Think about a situation in which you need to use that style. How could you go about developing that skill in order to solve that particular problem more effectively?

For example, I am not the most skilful of Analysts. I run my own business, and one area that has suffered as a result of my relative lack of strength as an Analyst is managing my accounts. I find it really hard to pay attention to detail, to remember the exceptions and cross-referencing, and all the other skills that help create an accurate, balanced set of accounts. So 'doing the books' has now become a deliberate development area. I enlist the help of my trusty accountant – who has designed excellent interactive spreadsheets for me – and I devote a certain amount of time each week to concentrated accounting work. I am slowly improving. But I am only doing so because I've chosen to and deliberately allocated time and mental resources to the task.

Looking at skills combinations

Effective problem-solving always involves a combination of styles. Solving a problem always means thinking at both Stage 1 and Stage 2. Intuitive problem-solving will tend to combine Explorer and Designer; rational problem-solving will tend to combine Analyst and Engineer. Really effective problem-solving will exploit the strengths of all four styles.

Two particular sets of combinations are worth thinking about.

First, the quality of our work at Stage 2 – when we're implementing a solution – depends directly on the quality of our work at Stage 1, when we're identifying the problem. Too little use of Analyst skills, for example, may mean that we're working with inaccurate information or faulty reasoning. Too little use of Explorer skills, on the other hand, may mean that we're seeking to solve a problem with too little information or analysis.

To see whether you favour Stage 1 or Stage 2, ask: does my profile sit more on the left or the right of the diagram?

For example, Figure 3.4 shows a profile that is quite strongly weighted towards Stage 2 problem-solving. This profile might suggest that the subject favours implementing solutions over understanding problems. More attention to Stage 1 problem-solving might help them develop more accurate and robust information on which to act.

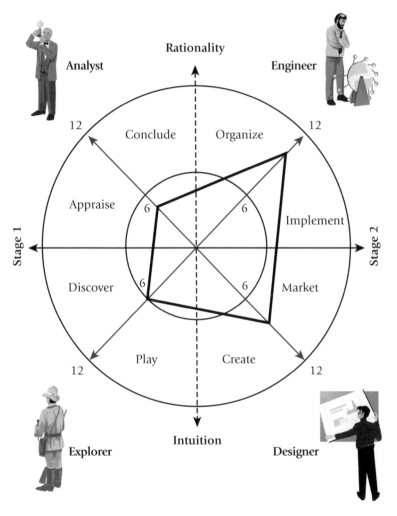

Figure 3.4 Sample profile: weighted towards Stage 2 problem-solving

Figure 3.5, by contrast, is a profile weighted towards Stage 1 problem-solving. This profile – particularly its emphasis on Explorer – suggests that the owner might benefit from more implementation skills: setting deadlines, testing ideas for feasibility, forcing themselves to make decisions.

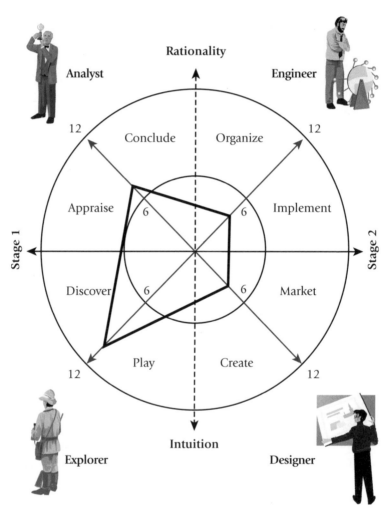

Figure 3.5 Sample profile: weighted towards Stage 1
problem-solving

Secondly, rationality is never divorced entirely from intuition. The skills of rational problem-solving – Analyst and Engineer skills – always operate on the back of the skills of intuitive problem-solving (Explorer and Designer). That's why I've put rationality *above* intuition in the diagram illustrating the four styles (see p. 63). Rational thinking always works with assumptions; in fact, it's not possible to think at all without making assumptions. Rational analysis always works with a selection of the information available to it; and it's intuition, more often than not, that made the selection.

Intuition can act without rationality (as we shall see, in the next chapter); but rationality can never act without some prior intuitive input.

To see whether your profile prefers intuition or rationality, ask: does my profile sit towards the top or the bottom of the diagram?

Figure 3.6 shows a profile weighted towards the intuitive. This profile suggests that its owner might need to develop more rational problem-solving skills: the skills of reasoning, argumentation and practical implementation that are represented by the top half of the profile.

By contrast, the profile in Figure 3.7 is weighted clearly towards rationality. The owner of this profile might benefit from working on some of the skills of intuitive problem-solving: exploring a little more, perhaps, and thinking more about the elegance of a solution than just its accuracy or practicality.

The virtues of versatility

Becoming a more versatile problem-solver means developing our skills, not becoming a different person. Versatility is a measure of our willingness and ability to change our behaviour, based on the needs of the situation or relationship at a particular time. Adapting your behaviour doesn't mean changing your personality.

You can choose which skills you want to develop. We often adapt our behaviour unconsciously, if the stakes aren't too high for us. We might be able to adapt easily to one problem, but not to another. We can test our ability to develop new problem-solving skills in situations where we may not *want* to adapt, but where we do *choose* to adapt.

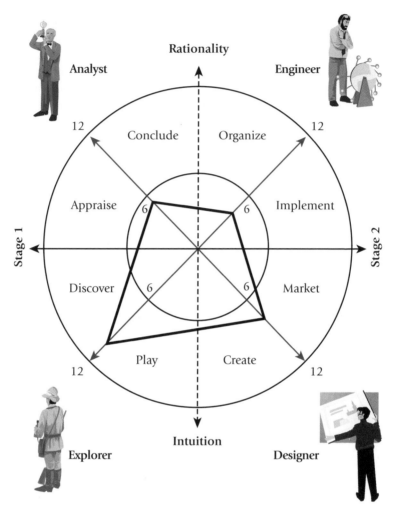

Figure 3.6 Sample profile: weighted towards the intuitive

No one style is naturally more versatile than another. Versatility may mean slowing down, or using more of the Analytical or Designer skills. It may mean moving more quickly into Explorer or Engineer mode. Analyst and Engineer usually benefit from developing interpersonal skills, and building relationships with others. Explorer and Designer often benefit from developing the more systematic skills of Analyst or Engineer.

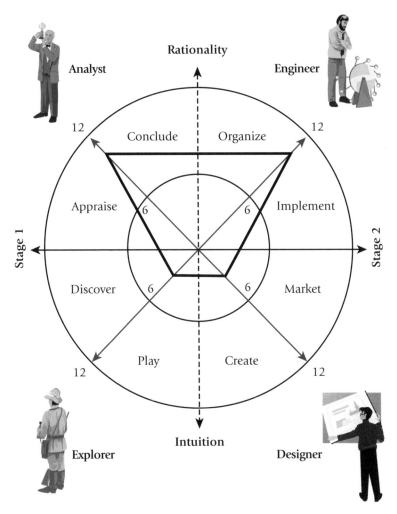

Figure 3.7 Sample profile: weighted towards rationality

It's easier to be versatile in some situations than in others. We often use one style in our professional lives and a different style in our personal or social lives. We may find ourselves less versatile when we're trying to solve problems with people we know well.

We need to decide how versatile we want to be. The temporary stress of using a 'foreign' problem-solving style may be worth it for the sake of improved results. Working a long way outside our comfort zone, however, may actually harm our effectiveness and do us little good. It's worth choosing our experiments in new problem-solving styles with some care.

There's no doubt, though, that by becoming more versatile problem-solvers, we increase our effectiveness generally. We can take more control over the issues that affect us, and increase our power to influence events. We can take fuller ownership of the problems we encounter.

And problem ownership is what we'll explore in the next chapter.

In brief

Becoming a better problem-solver means becoming more versatile.

We can identify four broad problem-solving styles:

- Analyst
- Explorer
- Engineer
- Designer.

Analyst and Explorer are the two styles of Stage 1 problem-solving: defining or describing problems.

Engineer and Designer are the two styles of Stage 2 problem-solving: generating solutions.

Analyst and Engineer are more rational styles, which tend to act *on* a situation.

Explorer and Designer are more intuitive styles, which tend to act *with* a situation.

Explorer's two key activities are discovering and playing.

Analyst's two key activities are appraising and concluding.

Engineer's two key activities are organizing and implementing.

Designer's two key activities are creating and marketing.

We can become more versatile by focusing on the styles that we're least comfortable with. We can explore whether we're more comfortable with intuitive or rational styles, and by understanding whether we favour Stage 1 or Stage 2 thinking. By developing different styles, we can become more versatile and more effective problem-solvers.

Chapter

Am I bothered? Blame, resistance and the call to ownership

Problems without owners, they say, usually become problems without solutions.

I think we use the word 'ownership' as a kind of shorthand for the way we relate to a problem. In this chapter, we'll look at four levels of ownership, and how each profoundly affects the way we go about solving a problem.

In and out of control

Our ownership of a problem increases when we feel more in control.

A sense of personal control is vital for our well-being. Without it we feel uncomfortable, and may start to feel ill. Control is what you lose when you're stuck in a traffic jam for no apparent reason. It's what we deny people when we put them in an old people's home or in prison. Control is what evaporates when you find yourself lost in a labyrinth of bureaucracy, or abandoned midway through a conversation with a distant call centre.

We can exert control in a situation by doing something: we can run away from a threat; store food for the future; modify our conditions to stay dry and warm. But we can also exert control mentally: if we *think* that we have some control, then we shall behave accordingly. If we *think* that we are helpless, we'll behave as if we *are* helpless.

The vital thing is to *feel* in control.

Circles of influence and circles of concern

Stephen Covey, in *Seven Habits of Highly Effective People*, models this idea of personal control by drawing two circles, one within the other. The outer circle he calls the circle of concern: it contains all the problems we worry about, but which are outside our control (things, in his words, such as 'the national debt, terrorism, the weather'). Within the circle of concern is the circle of influence: in this circle are all the problems over which we feel a sense of control (see Figure 4.1).

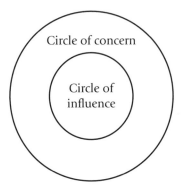

Figure 4.1 Circles of influence and concern

Covey suggests that we can respond to problems reactively or proactively:

- We react to a problem in our circle of concern: we assume that we can't change the problem itself because we feel that we can't control it.
- We act proactively to a problem in our circle of influence: our sense of control over the situation leads us to engage with the problem and try to change it.

We *choose* to put problems into one circle or the other. 'Our behaviour,' says Covey, 'is a function of our decisions, not our conditions.'

Being more effective, according to Covey, means paying attention to the right problems. It means concentrating on the problems we can control, and not on the ones we can't. Being more effective means increasing our circle of influence (see Figure 4.2).

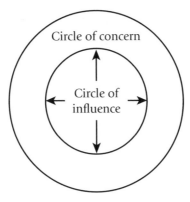

Figure 4.2 Increasing the circle of influence

Concern, influence and ownership

We can use Covey's two circles to understand problem ownership. At the outer edge of our circle of concern, we feel no ownership; at the centre of our circle of influence, we experience complete ownership (see Figure 4.3).

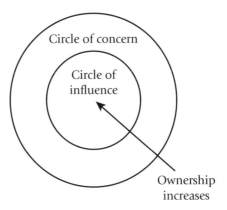

Figure 4.3 Increasing ownership

When do we place problems in our circle of concern? Perhaps we are affected by a problem but can't understand it (like a banking crisis or global climate change). Perhaps we feel we lack the power to influence it (imagine being an employee in an organization facing meltdown as the result of a strategic error). We may feel deeply moved by a problem but unable to act (as when we see pictures of famine in a distant land).

And when do we place problems in our circle of influence? When we feel that we *understand* the problem adequately; and when we feel that we have all that is necessary to *act* to solve the problem.

What to do

Concern or influence?

Take a large piece of paper and draw the two circles on it. Think about some problems you are currently facing and write each one on a sticky note. Place the sticky notes in one of the two circles, depending on how much influence you feel you have over the problem.

Compare a problem in one circle with a problem in the other. What's the difference? List the factors that affect your thinking about each problem.

Now pick up one of the problems in your circle of concern. Do you want to move the problem into your circle of influence? What would need to change in order for that problem to go into the circle of influence? What would you need to *do*? What *can* you do?

Four levels of ownership

The four levels of problem ownership are:

1. blame,
2. resistance,
3. responsibility,
4. commitment.

At each level, we feel different degrees of control over the problem. And the action we take will differ accordingly.

But here's the most important idea in this chapter:

We choose the way we own a problem. And the choice we make can transform the problem itself.

Blame

Blame is the lowest level of ownership. In fact, on this level, ownership is pretty well zero.

Blame is probably one of the most common responses to problems. (How many of us work in a 'blame culture'?) And we all know how debilitating blame can be, especially to our ability to solve problems. So we need to take a long, hard look at blame: what it is, how it arises, how it perpetuates itself and how to avoid it.

We can represent this level of ownership as an arrow in the circle of concern, pointing outwards (see Figure 4.4). The arrow is in our circle of concern because blame is a *reaction* to a situation over which we have no control. And it points outwards because, when we feel powerless, one of our most powerful urges is to shift ownership of the problem *away* from us.

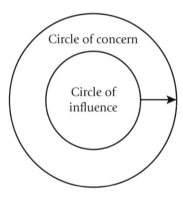

Figure 4.4 Blame

The origins of blame

Blame is our natural response to feeling out of control.

Intuitive problem-solving works by matching an external stimulus to a mental model. If we can't pattern-match – because a problem is complex, perhaps, or we can't see what caused it – we feel out of control. The best way to regain that control is to find a credible pattern-match. And the way we do that is interesting. Our minds default to a position in which we believe that someone – or something – has created the problem *deliberately*. That pattern-match then gives us a clear action as a solution: punish the perpetrator.

And that's how blame is born.

What's interesting about blame is that we use it even when there's obviously nobody to blame. We shout at the dog when it 'refuses' to obey; we kick a burst tyre. Blame sees no difference between people, animals and inanimate objects. In blame mode, we assume that *everything* we come into contact with is like us: human.

The principle seems to be:

When no cause is discernable, assume personal intent.

Blame is a form of magical thinking. When we feel powerless, we begin to see meanings and intentions where none exist. Blame operates like pareidolia, which we looked at in Chapter 1: stressed out by uncertainty, we start ascribing malign intentions to our partners, or to the people we work with. We hatch conspiracy theories. We blame our managers, the government, the gods, or fate.

Moving beyond blame

How do we escape the blame cycle? The first thing to do is recognize what we're doing. We should acknowledge that blaming is a natural, intuitive response to feeling out of control. But rational problem-solving can also tell us that blame is almost never helpful as a way to approach a problem: it damages others, and it can damage us by perpetuating a sense of helplessness.

So, after recognizing what we're doing, we can challenge our behaviour – and change it.

What to do

If you are blaming someone for a problem:

- Challenge your reasons for blaming. Stop generalizing: what makes this situation different?
- Stop using blaming solutions: making life difficult for the other person, refusing to help, copying senior management into your emails ...
- Separate the problem from the person. Tell them that you are doing so.
- Agree with the person that a problem exists. Agree a definition of the problem.
- Discuss who should take ownership.
- Offer help.

If you are being blamed for a problem:

- Separate the problem from yourself.
- Lower your emotional arousal before responding.
- Decide whether you are responsible for the problem's existence.
- Look for help: someone who can see the problem objectively from the outside.
- Discuss the problem with the person you think is blaming you (after all, they may not be blaming you, and you may be misreading the situation).
- Decide the appropriate response: to hand over the problem, to take responsibility for the problem, or to commit to constructing a solution.

And what if you are unlucky enough to be working in a blame culture? Can you avoid being infected? It may be hard, but you can decide not to contribute to it. You can choose your conversations – whether to take part in the gossip and the backbiting, or avoid it. You can choose whether to challenge blaming behaviour or simply avoid becoming involved.

Above all, you can follow Stephen Covey's advice and concentrate on the problems where you have some control. You can seek to increase your circle of influence.

Resistance

Resistance is the second level of ownership. Like blame, resistance *reacts* to a sense of powerlessness. Unlike blame, however, resistance includes the *desire* to do something, to take control. Without the desire, what are we resisting? It's the friction between that desire and some other internal force that causes the resistance.

Resistance is represented in the circle of concern as an arrow pointing inwards (see Figure 4.5). The arrow remains in your circle of concern because you feel you have no influence, but it's pointing inwards because you do want to act. You want to take ownership of the problem, but something is stopping you.

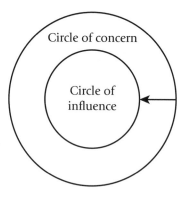

Figure 4.5 Resistance

Resistance, like blame, is a natural response to uncertainty. Unlike blame, however, resistance is static rather than active. Blame strikes out; resistance digs its heels in. Blame discharges stress; resistance increases it. Blame damages others; when we resist, we risk damaging ourselves.

Some forms of resistance are relatively minor: we've all put off the moment when we need to start work on a project or bring up an awkward issue with a colleague. Sometimes we engage in 'avoidance behaviours': making another cup of tea rather than making a difficult call; leaving the office rather than confronting a painful decision.

But resistance can go deeper, towards denial. And denial may offer a respite from stress. But persistent denial of a persistent problem is hardly going to help us solve it.

What to do

Recognizing resistance

Here are some of the key symptoms of resistance. Identify the last time you found yourself exhibiting one or more of them:

- **Procrastination:** putting off the moment when we need to start working on a problem; failing to turn up for meetings.
- **Avoidance behaviours:** finding something else to do rather than buckling down.
- **Denial:** failing to answer the phone or emails; missing appointments.
- **Malicious compliance:** being late for meetings; carrying out instructions to the mere letter; assigning a subordinate a task that undermines action to solve the problem.

'Out of procedure'

We often resist when we're wrenched 'out of procedure'.

Imagine that you have spent some time learning how to operate a new computer program. You attended training sessions; you practised regularly; it wasn't easy, but in the past few weeks you've finally mastered the skills and you are now 'up to speed'.

This morning, an email appears from the IT department, telling you that the system is being abandoned in favour of a different one.

My guess is that your first response will be resistance: 'Certainly not! After all that effort? If they think I'm going to change *again*, and go through that hell – they can think again ....'

We use procedural memory, as we saw in Chapter 2, to learn new skills (like operating that computer program). Procedural memories have two important characteristics:

1. They must be repeated many times before they become ingrained: we have to practise.
2. Once they are embedded, they are more or less permanent. Even if you don't ride a bicycle for years, you will undoubtedly remember how to do it after a few moments.

These two features mean that procedural memories *resist* being modified or removed. This resistance makes sense. It's energy-efficient: we don't have to waste energy relearning what we already know.

The more solidly imprinted the procedural memory, the more resistant we are to modifying or replacing it. If a problem disrupts a procedural memory you've built up over years, the resistance may be considerable. Remember the resistance that met the idea of decimal currency or metric measures? (Some of us remember!)

What to do

What's the procedure?

If a problem is causing resistance, it may mean that some deeply rooted procedural memory is being challenged.

Identify that procedural memory and you may be able to begin managing your resistance – which is the first step towards taking greater ownership of the problem.

What need is not being met?

A problem can also provoke resistance if it threatens a fundamental need.

We all have obvious physical needs. All human beings need breathable air, clean water, nutritious food, exercise, sensory stimulation, shelter and sleep. Any attempt to withdraw those resources can trigger resistance: a fact exploited by interrogation techniques such as sleep deprivation or waterboarding.

But we also have emotional needs, which must be met if we are to be healthy, functioning, effective people. We're just as likely to resist a threat to one of these needs as we are to resist the threat of drowning or starving. One such emotional need, as we've seen, is the need for a sense of personal control. If a problem makes us feel powerless, we're very likely to resist tackling it. And we're also likely to resist if one of the following needs is threatened:

- security – a safe place that allows us to live and develop fully;
- attention – both from and to other people;
- emotional intimacy – knowing that at least one person accepts us for what we are;
- feeling part of a community – a family, tribe, ethnic group or nation;
- privacy – the opportunity to be alone to reflect on our experiences and make sense of them;
- a sense of status in a social group – a feeling that others value us;
- a sense of competence and achievement – that we are good at something and have made a difference somewhere;
- meaning and purpose in our lives – which may come from other people, from a belief system or from being stretched in what we do or think.

(This list of human needs derives from the work of Joe Griffin and Ivan Tyrrell.)

Resistance might be a sign that we feel a problem threatens one or more of these needs. We might find ourselves able to take greater ownership of the problem *if* the need could be met or guaranteed.

What to do

Meeting the need

Identify the need that is not being met, and you may have discovered the source of your resistance.

- **Security:** does the prospect of tackling the problem make you feel unsafe?

▶

- **Attention:** do you feel that you are not being acknowledged for your efforts in tackling the problem?

- **Emotional intimacy:** does the problem threaten your need for acceptance or love?

- **Feeling part of a community:** would dealing with the problem alienate you from your team or workmates?

- **Privacy:** does the problem expose some aspect of your life you wish to remain private?

- **A sense of status in a social group:** do you feel exploited in being asked to deal with the problem?

- **A sense of competence and achievement:** do you feel incapable of tackling the problem, not up to the task or afraid of failing?

- **Meaning and purpose in our lives:** perhaps the problem is deflecting you from what you really want to do, achieve or work for?

Reducing resistance

Different features of a problem will affect how much we resist tackling it:

- **Is the problem controllable?** We resist when we lack power to influence a situation – when a problem is in our circle of concern.

- **How serious is the problem?** We may resist the need to repair a leaking roof less than we resist the need to move house.

- **How long-lasting is the problem?** We resist long-term problems more than short-term ones. Indeed, our resistance may make a problem persist for longer. We may resist solving a difficult Sudoku puzzle less than we resist tackling a chronic problem such as a disintegrating relationship, debt or addiction.

- **When has the problem occurred?** We may resist less if the problem finds us at a good moment for solving it; we may resist more if we're oppressed with a dozen other problems at the same moment.

- **How predictable is the problem?** If we can see a problem coming and plan for it, we may resist less. Surprises will probably trigger considerable resistance.

All other things being equal (which they never are), our resistance to a problem is likely to decrease if we can make the problem more controllable, less serious, more immediate or urgent and less surprising. If we can choose the moment to tackle the problem, so much the better.

Taking ownership of a problem

Recall Steven Covey's advice. Effective people concentrate on their circle of influence. They focus their attention and energy on the problems over which they have some control, rather than the problems in their circle of concern.

Neither blame nor resistance helps you to solve problems. They might briefly make you feel better; but, if you truly want to solve the problem, you need to bring it within your circle of influence.

Moving a problem into your circle of influence may not be easy. How hard can it be to stop the virus of blame from infecting our view of a problem? (Consider employees who have been made redundant; partners going through a messy separation; communities locked in decades of mutual distrust and violence.) How difficult can it be to overcome our resistance to tackling a problem? (Ask a recovering addict, a reformed criminal or someone courageously battling disease or disability.) We should acknowledge that blame and resistance are natural responses to problems. But we are human beings; we can choose what to do.

The first step is to change the way we look at a problem. And we have many resources to help us do that.

What to do

Breaking out of blame or resistance

It's all very well saying that we should stop blaming or resisting. But how can we *do* that?

Here's a simple technique that's guaranteed to get some kind of result. We'll be looking at it in more detail later, but it might be useful to introduce it right now – as first aid to help you overcome blame or resistance.

The technique is this:

> *Express the problem as a phrase beginning with the words 'how to'.*

And – um – that's it. I said it was simple.

But notice what happens when we express the problem as a 'how to'. Instantly, the problem is no longer something wrong but something we are thinking about doing. The focus is no longer on the situation, and instead is on what you can do – it enables you to start to take ownership of the problem.

'How to' is a remarkable technique. We'll find out a lot more about it in Chapter 8.

Responsibility

Responsibility is the third level of ownership. On this level, we have moved from *reacting* to a problem towards taking a *proactive* approach to it. With responsibility, we have activated our desire to act on a problem.

Responsibility is ownership of a problem conferred on you by others. You can represent responsibility as an arrow in your circle of influence, pointing outwards (see Figure 4.6). The arrow is in your circle of influence because you feel you can take action on the problem; it's pointing outwards because your sense of responsibility is towards another person, or to other people.

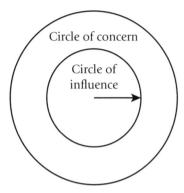

Figure 4.6 Responsibility

Responsibility and presented problems

It's at this level of ownership that problem-solving proper begins. Once you take the problem into your circle of influence, you begin to assume some level of control over the problem. When you take responsibility for a problem, you feel that the problem has been presented to you and it's your task to deal with it. So I call problems on this level of ownership *presented problems*.

Presented problems: key characteristics

- They happen to us. We aren't responsible for their existence. (So they are not our 'fault'.)

- They are usually expressed as a statement about what is wrong.

- We see them as an obstacle in our path.

- There is a perceived gap between what *is* and what *should be*.

- Solving them involves *effort*.

My guess is that most of the situations we regard as problems are presented problems. Most of the tasks on a 'to-do' list – all the chores of an ordinary working day – are likely to be presented problems. They're problems for which you take responsibility, but you might see them as obstacles stopping you from doing what you *really* want to do.

Because presented problems are your responsibility, one of your main priorities might be to discharge that responsibility as efficiently as possible. You want to cross the problem off your 'to-do' list, get it out of the way and move on. Once you've solved it, you'd prefer a presented problem not to re-appear. You may well find yourself, therefore, wanting to 'fix' presented problems: to look for the solution that removes the problem permanently. Unfortunately, one presented problem may well be followed by another; and before you know it, you're 'fire-fighting'.

You may work in an organization where fire-fighting is accepted as the norm. Most organizations, after all, have more problems than people to deal with them. If responsibilities aren't managed properly, problems will be 'patched' – in other words, temporarily fixed – while everyone learns to juggle ever more furiously. Managers who patch and juggle well may be highly praised; but such heroics can carry a heavy cost in terms of increased stress, burnout – and fewer problems actually solved.

What to do

Do you work in a fire-fighting culture?

Tick the boxes that apply to your organization.

- [ ] We have more problems than problem-solvers.
- [ ] Many problems are patched rather than solved.
- [ ] Many patched problems create new problems.
- [ ] Many patched problems recur and need re-patching.
- [ ] We regularly interrupt long-term work to address urgent problems.
- [ ] We often solve problems at the last minute, using heroic efforts that are highly applauded.
- [ ] Fire-fighting causes drops in levels of performance.
- [ ] Fire-fighting creates stress among staff.
- [ ] Many people here would say that fire-fighting is a core feature of their work.

☐ The CEO and other senior managers are continually juggling and changing priorities.

☐ We run 'away days', retreats or long all-staff events to focus on long-term problems, but rarely implement the solutions.

If you've ticked two or more statements, fire-fighting is probably a feature of your organization's culture. If you've ticked three or more, it's probably endemic.

You may not be able to change your organization's culture. But you can start looking after yourself – and you may need to do so, for your own well-being. Take charge of your responsibilities and manage them more effectively.

Responsibility as a contract

Responsibility is always socially determined. To have a responsibility is to have an obligation to another person, to a group or to society. After all, it's other people who hold us responsible for our actions. To carry out your responsibilities is to deserve praise or reward; if you fail to discharge them, you can expect to be criticized or punished.

To be responsible is to enter into a kind of contract. Indeed, we often use the language of commercial or legal obligation to explain our responsibilities. We might speak of *honouring* our responsibilities, for example, in the same way that we must honour a bargain. We *discharge* a responsibility, in the same way that we might discharge a debt. To be *accountable* means that someone can hold us to account for our responsibilities: that we may have to pay, literally or metaphorically, if we fail to discharge them. Indeed, we might say that we're *liable* for the responsibilities we take on; that liability is a measure of the extent of our responsibility, or of the price we might have to pay for failing to honour it.

Responsibilities, like all contracts, have limits. Once you've discharged your responsibilities, paid your liabilities, done what you're accountable for, your ownership ceases – and you can walk away.

Taking on a responsibility, like signing a contract, must be a free act. To be truly responsible for tackling a problem, you must be free and able to choose what to do. To be compelled against your will to do something arguably absolves you of responsibility: hence the appeal by those who claim, after committing horrific acts, that they 'were just following orders'.

But freedom is as much psychological as political. Free will is the essence of responsibility. To be *responsible for one's actions* is to know what one is doing, to be able to reflect on that action – and to be able to choose not to do it. Indeed, the law assumes that some people – the young or the mentally ill, for example – can't take responsibility for their own actions, and therefore can't be held legally responsible for any criminal acts they commit.

Taking on a responsibility, therefore, carries with it a paradox. On the one hand, a responsibility is a duty or an obligation towards others; on the other, it's something we take on freely, by our own choice.

We live this paradox every day. If a manager, a teacher, or a parent complains about the weight of their responsibilities, they are likely to be told: 'Why complain? You chose these responsibilities; you made a contract; you're enjoying the benefits that come with the job. You're free to walk away.' Which may, or may not, be true. Our choices carry consequences, some of which we may not be able to escape.

The perils of responsibility

Taking responsibility for a problem brings inevitable risks. We're taking on a problem on behalf of somebody else; we're agreeing to honour an obligation without having been entirely free to define it. As a result, problems for which we take responsibility often share certain troubling features:

- **Unclear goals.** The person handing responsibility to you may not know precisely what they want you to do, or – even more troublingly – what they *don't* want you to do. A problem might start small and grow unexpectedly; it might start simple and get horribly complicated.

- **Lack of control.** If we had complete influence over what to do and how to do it, we'd be happier. But your obligations to others may limit the control you can exercise.

- **Lack of immediate feedback.** You may have to check with others about aspects of the problem: information, deadlines or criteria of success. And those people may be unavailable.

- **A mismatch between challenge and skill.** You often have to assume responsibility for problems that are trivially easy, boring and tedious (call them chores). You may have to take responsibility for problems that are mind-numbingly difficult (we'll call them headaches in the next chapter). And you can't simply ignore your responsibilities just because they're tedious chores or stressful headaches.

- **Distractions.** The working day's full of them. It's often impossible to concentrate on one task at a time. When was the last time you completed a job without being interrupted by another?

- **You're accountable.** Your child expects dinner to be on the table. The customer needs an answer. Your manager is waiting for the quarterly figures.

- **You have to think about causes and consequences.** How did the problem get this complicated? Do I have authority to do what I want to do? What if ...?

- **You're pressed for time.** Every new problem is another demand on your time. It's hard to concentrate if you're clock-watching.

- **What's in it for me?** If you can see a clear reward at the end of the job, you might feel better. When were you last thanked for solving a problem? And is solving this problem part of your job description, anyway?

Given all these complexities, it would hardly be surprising if you found yourself resisting your responsibilities, or lapsing into fire-fighting.

What to do

Setting the bounds of responsibility

Think of a responsibility as being like a contract. The best way to honour a responsibility is to know beforehand precisely what you're taking on. One way to clarify all this is to use Rudyard Kipling's famous serving men: the six Ws:

1 **Why?** What's the overall objective in tackling this problem? What outcome are you being expected to achieve? Do you have SMART goals (are they specific, measurable, achievable, realistic and timely)?

2 **Who?** To whom are you accountable? And for whom are you accountable?

3 **What?** What precisely is the problem you're taking on? How well do you understand it? How well defined is it? (The analytical tools we'll examine in the next chapter will be critically important in answering these questions.) What actions are you being called upon to carry out – exactly?

4 **When?** Is there a deadline? Are there milestones that you will be expected to hit?

5 **Where?** Where will your solution have an impact? How far does your responsibility stretch? Where are its boundaries or limits?

6 **How?** What authority have you been granted? What are you permitted to do – and what do you need to ask further permission to do? What constraints will you be expected to operate under? What resources are available to you? What support can you count on?

Commitment

Commitment is the fourth and highest level of problem ownership. On this level, the problem is so firmly within our circle of influence that we feel we've created the problem ourselves: we're responsible for its very existence.

Commitment can be represented in your circle of influence, as an arrow pointing inwards (see Figure 4.7). The arrow is in your circle of influence because you have complete control over the problem – including how it's defined, and what you choose to do. The arrow points inwards because your ownership of the problem is complete and unconditional.

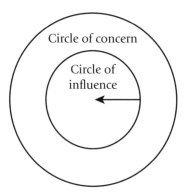

Figure 4.7 Commitment

Problems at this level of ownership are the problems you want to have. They are the problems you leap out of bed to solve. It might be winning a sailing race on a windless day; it might be painting the sunset before it fades; and, yes, it might be catching that potential customer before the competition gets there. Indeed, you may feel that you've actually brought the problem into existence yourself: you've set yourself the problem and you'll stop at nothing until you've solved it. For this reason, I call problems at this level of ownership *constructed problems*.

Commitment and constructed problems

Constructed problems are the problems we search out, the problems we choose, the problems we create. We might not even call them problems – we might call them challenges or projects. A constructed problem isn't so much an obstacle on our path as the reason for taking the journey. Constructed problems 'turn us on'.

Constructed problems: key characteristics

- We create them. They didn't exist until we thought of them. We are responsible for their existence.

- They can be expressed as a phrase beginning with the words 'how to'.

- We see them as the reason for doing something.

- There is a perceived gap between what *is* and what *could be*.

- Solving them is *energizing*.

Solving a presented problem is discharging a responsibility; solving a constructed problem is an end in itself. Presented problems are goal-oriented: we solve them in order to achieve some other objective. Constructed problems, in contrast, are *autotelic*: they're worth solving for their own sake.

Finding the flow state

When you commit fully to a constructed problem, you might find yourself in a heightened mental state. You might talk about being 'totally immersed' in the problem, or being 'in the zone'. The condition has been investigated in great depth by the psychologist Mihály Csíkszentmihályi, who famously calls it 'flow'.

Csíkszentmihályi (his surname is pronounced 'chicks send me high-ee') began to study the phenomenon in the 1960s. He observed artists while they painted, fascinated by the concentration with which they worked. He was prompted to ask: what is happiness? What do we feel when we're happy? Why do some activities make us happy when others don't? How could we increase our stock of happiness?

He spent the next 30 years investigating these questions, looking at people around the world: elderly Korean women, Navajo shepherds, Japanese teenage motorcycle gang members, assembly-line workers in Chicago. What motivated these people was the quality of the experience they had while doing what they did: an experience characterized by joy, concentration, a sense of mastery and a lack of self-consciousness. It was an experience that 'took them out of themselves'; they felt that they had grown as a result of it.

And it was this experience that Csíkszentmihályi called 'flow'. Flow, he says, is 'the way people describe their state of mind when consciousness is harmoniously ordered'. Csíkszentmihályi noticed that the flow experience had a number of consistent features:

- **Loss of self-consciousness.** People took no account of how others saw them. Their attention was solely on what they were doing.
- **Action merges with awareness.** People took no account of the past or the future. The possibility of failure didn't occur to them. They were living and working entirely in the present.
- **A distorted sense of time.** As the saying goes, 'time flies when you're having fun'.
- **Intrinsic reward.** There was no thought for any compensation, payment or recognition for the work.

This 'optimal experience', as he called it, didn't happen when people were relaxing; and it certainly didn't happen when they were consuming food, alcohol or drugs. Instead, it seemed to require an activity that stretched their capacities – something difficult, risky or even painful. The task usually involved discovery, novelty or creativity. And it was something people *chose* to do.

In other words, they were tackling a constructed problem.

Now, tackling a constructed problem may not guarantee you the legal high of the flow experience. But it probably will do so if a number of key elements are in place:

- **Clear goals**. You know what you want to achieve and you know that you can achieve it.
- **Control.** You feel that you're completely in charge of what you're doing.
- **Immediate feedback.** Success and failure at any point are vividly clear, so that you can adjust your behaviour quickly.

- **A balance between challenge and skill.** You feel that what you're doing is neither too hard nor too easy.
- **Concentration**. Your attention is focused exclusively on the task in hand.

Flow is good for us. It produces intense feelings of satisfaction and enjoyment. Flow improves our performance and helps us develop our skills. Flow motivates us to grow in competence and self-esteem. All of which must be good for our health.

How can we increase our commitment?

Life can never be wholly a matter of following our commitments. We all have responsibilities that we must discharge: presented problems that we must deal with.

And our sense of problem ownership can shift. A constructed problem can easily become a presented problem. What started out as an exciting challenge can become a burden; you can become distracted, lose your sense of mastery or control in the situation. But, by the same token, you can choose to transform some presented problems into constructed problems. In fact, just about any activity can be made autotelic. As Csíkszentmihályi said in an interview:

❝Talking to a friend, reading to a child, playing with a pet, or mowing the lawn can each produce flow, provided you find the challenge in what you are doing and then focus on doing it as best you can.**❞**

Flow, then, isn't something that happens to us; it's something we can make happen. If you can influence your ability to focus, to concentrate, to set yourself goals or seek feedback on your performance, you can turn some of your responsibilities into commitments and take fuller ownership of the problem.

'In many ways,' says Csíkszentmihályi, 'the secret to a happy life is to learn to get flow from as many of the things we have to do as possible.'

In brief

'Ownership' is shorthand for the way we relate to a problem. Our sense of ownership increases as we feel more in control.

We can identify four levels of ownership:

1 blame,

2 resistance,

3 responsibility,

4 commitment.

Blame and resistance tend to arise when a problem is in your circle of concern. Responsibility and commitment tend to arise when a problem is in your circle of influence.

Blame is a reaction to feeling out of control. Its guiding principle is: *when no cause is discernable, assume personal intent.*

To escape the blame cycle: recognize what you're doing; use rational problem-solving to change your sense of ownership.

Resistance is also a reaction to feeling out of control. We often resist when we're wrenched 'out of procedure'. A problem can also provoke resistance if it threatens a fundamental need.

We resist less if a problem is controllable, minor, immediate or urgent and unsurprising.

Responsibility is ownership of a problem conferred on us by others. At the level of responsibility, we see problems as presented.

To be responsible is to enter into a kind of contract. The best way to honour a responsibility is to clarify it precisely, using Kipling's famous serving men: the six Ws.

Commitment is a proactive stance, in which we choose or even create a problem. Problems at this level of ownership are constructed.

Committing fully to a problem puts us into a 'flow' state. You can create the 'flow' state: if you can focus more, set yourself goals or seek feedback on your performance, you can turn some of your responsibilities into commitments.

Puzzle, headache, plan, dream: four types of problem

Let's recap what we've learnt so far about our skills as problem-solvers. Armed with your knowledge and new skills, you can begin to look at different types of problem, using a systematic method.

Problem-solving: the story so far

Here are the main points we've covered thus far in the book.

Having a problem means being stuck

You know you've got a problem when you want to do something, but you don't know what to do.

Most problem-solving is intuitive

We match information from our experience to mental patterns, either inherited or learned. The pattern-match tells us what to do.

When intuitive problem-solving breaks down, problem-solving becomes a task with two stages

We notice that we have a problem only when this pattern-matching fails to tell us what to do. When this happens, and we become stuck, the intuitive pattern-matching approach splits into two stages: Stage 1, at which we examine and identify the problem; and Stage 2, where we decide what to do.

We can use both intuitive and rational problem-solving to solve problems

Intuitive problem-solving can help us look at problems in different ways, by reframing and switching contexts. Rational problem-solving uses reasoning, logic and evaluation to examine the situation, gather evidence, challenge our mental models, identify options for action and work out what to do.

Intuitive problem-solving and rational problem-solving operate in a close and sometimes challenging relationship. We can solve problems intuitively without engaging in rational problem-solving, but rational problem-solving cannot operate without some intuitive input. All thinking is based on assumptions, and assumptions – by definition – are intuitive. Indeed, one of the most important parts of rational problem-solving is challenging the assumptions with which we view a problem.

Four sets of skills help us solve problems

At Stage 1, the **Explorer** and **Analyst** styles help us identify the problem. The Explorer style helps us intuitively to see a problem more richly, and the Analyst style helps us rationally to understand it more accurately and objectively.

At Stage 2, the **Engineer** and **Designer** styles help us to decide what to do: the Engineer style by helping us construct feasible solutions, and the Designer style by helping us create more elegant ones.

Ownership of a problem can take two forms

- **Responsibility** is problem ownership conferred on us by others: they, not we, are responsible for the form of the problem, the restraints and constraints that govern it and our authority to deal with it.

- **Commitment** is full, unconditional ownership of a problem; we are entirely free to define the problem and to manage how we deal with it.

We can divide all problems into presented problems and constructed problems

A problem becomes a presented problem if we express it as a **statement of what's wrong:**

The car won't start.

Sales are down this quarter.

Students are profoundly disengaged from the learning process.

A problem becomes a constructed problem if we express it as a **phrase beginning with the words 'how to':**

How to start the car.

How to improve sales next quarter.

How to engage students' interest in learning.

Constructed problems	Presented problems
'What do I want to achieve?' Made by us We are responsible for creating them The reason for taking the journey Perceived gap: what is/what could be Cause creative tension *Solution: dispel tension by releasing energy*	*'What's wrong?'* Happen to us Not our 'fault' but we are responsible for solving them Obstacle in our path Perceived gap: what is/what should be Cause stress *Solution: fight or flight*
Examples:	**Examples:**
Gaining a qualification Improving quality Working out a strategy Innovating a new product or service Increasing market share	The photocopier breaking down A new product invading our market Being stuck in a traffic jam Delays in a production process

The really important point here is that a problem is either presented or constructed *because we see it that way*. The terms are distinctions of definition, not of objective truth. The only real distinction between a presented and a constructed problem is in the way we express it.

And that means we can change the way we look at a problem.

In fact, presented and constructed problems often morph into each other. How often have you committed excitedly to the new challenge of a constructed problem ('I can do that!'), only to find within a few days that you're stressed out facing a mountain of presented problems. Perhaps, less obviously, the transformation can happen in the other direction. You may have been presented with an onerous task, only to find that it grows, as you become more interested, into an intriguing challenge.

Well-structured and ill-structured problems

So far, then, we've distinguished problems as presented or constructed. Another way to distinguish them is in terms of their *structure*.

We can define a problem's structure by looking at four key elements:

1. initial conditions (where we are);
2. goal conditions (where we want to be);
3. operators (the different ways in which we can get from initial conditions to goal conditions);
4. constraints (whatever limits our action).

Two kinds of constraints

Constraints come in two forms. Some constraints are things we *can't* do. Others are things we *must* do. When considering constraints, we need to consider both.

Some constraints will be codified in manuals, regulations and laws. Others will be tacit: social conventions, morals, matters of conscience. The trickiest constraints we face are the ones inside our own heads: the assumptions that unnecessarily limit the way we see a problem.

(Thanks to Fred Nickols for this useful distinction.)

If a problem's four elements are clear to us, we can call the problem *well structured*. If one or more of the elements is unclear, the problem becomes *ill structured*.

Well-structured problems

Solving a jigsaw puzzle is a good example of a well-structured problem:

- Initial conditions are clear. (All the pieces are jumbled up in the box.)
- Goal conditions are clear. (The lid of the box shows the finished picture.)
- Operators are clear. (Sort the pieces, find straight edges and corners, solve small areas of the puzzle and link them together ...)
- Constraints are clear. (There is only one correct arrangement of the pieces; no cutting or folding the pieces; no colouring of the pieces; no substituting pieces from another puzzle ...)

It's hard, in theory, to imagine how we could get seriously stuck solving a jigsaw puzzle. As long as all four elements remain clear, we should be able to solve the problem by simply applying the operators for as long as it takes.

Of course, in reality we can get stuck doing a jigsaw. When that happens, we can usually determine how the problem has become ill structured by investigating the four key structural elements of the problem. Perhaps we have too many pieces of the same colour, or we don't know whether some pieces are missing (initial conditions less clear); perhaps we've lost the box lid carrying the picture (goal conditions less clear). Perhaps there is some trick in the jigsaw's design that frustrates our operators: the puzzle is circular and has a border of one colour; the edges of the puzzle are not smooth but shaped exactly like the interlocking pegs of internal pieces ...

Ill-structured problems

Deciding where to go out for the day is a good example of an ill-structured problem. Initial conditions are probably more or less clear: you know where you are at the moment, and your current circumstances don't count as a day out. (But think about it: could you somehow transform your current circumstances into a day out without going out?) Goal conditions, on the other hand, are unclear: you could go anywhere for a day out.

How might you solve such a problem? You could load your partner and children into the car and just set out. On your journey, you might see a good place to have a picnic and decide to buy your food and drink nearby. You might see a theme park that would distract the children (or the partner) for a couple of hours and then decide whether to visit, on the basis of cost, time restraints and your previous experience of theme parks. And so on.

An alternative to this spontaneous, improvised solution would be to examine more closely all the structural elements of the problem *except* the goal conditions:

- **Initial conditions**. Where are we now? What's within reach? What resources are available to us?

- **Operators**. What kind of transport is available? What could we use?

- **Constraints**. Who do we have to take? What do they like doing? What don't they enjoy doing? Do we have to take the dog? How long have we got? How much do we want to spend? What's the weather like?

Now we need two things: information and the ability to recognize a satisfactory solution. Gathering knowledge and fitting it to the structural elements of the problem creates a solution.

Solving an ill-structured problem, then, means increasing our ownership of the problem. We must bring the problem further into our circle of influence. As we saw in the last chapter, doing so means either:

- clarifying our responsibility; or
- becoming committed to solving the problem.

One way or another, we shall need to define the problem more clearly. And we can do *that* by:

- specifying more clearly any or all of the problem's structural elements;
- gathering information about the situation; or
- looking out for a goal state that we can recognize as satisfactory.

We could imagine applying this technique to the problem of the day out. Mum lists all the structural elements of the problem; Dad is banished to the computer to gather useful information; children are asked to think up as many solutions as they can.

By a process of collaborative brainstorming, a plan is hatched.

It might just happen.

Structure and stuckness

It's easy enough to see how an ill-structured problem creates stuckness. And stuckness, as we've seen, can provoke an emotional reaction or trigger the stress response. Faced with an ill-structured problem, we're likely to resort to an intuitive solution: a 'shot in the dark' or a wild guess. Or we might give up and collapse into despondency or learned helplessness.

By attending to the structure of the problem, we can generate a better solution.

Some ill-structured problems can be 'tamed': you might be able to improve the structure of the problem by defining one or more variables more clearly. Simplifying the problem is often a viable way towards a solution. But sometimes a problem's structure is overwhelmingly complex or ambiguous, and it can't be 'tamed'. As we'll see in Chapter 7, we can call such problems 'wicked'; and they demand more wholesale transformation.

But well-structured problems can create stuckness too. A problem may be so well structured that only one solution seems possible: and if we find that solution unacceptable – we're stuck. (Remember the curse of the right answer, which we investigated in Chapter 1?)

If you want to find an acceptable solution to rigidly well-structured problems, you may have to deliberately *loosen* the problem's structure.

- **Initial conditions**. Is there another way of looking at the situation? How would someone else see it?
- **Goal conditions**. Is the specified goal actually the only possible goal? Could you alter the measures of success or think of an alternative workable solution?
- **Operators**. Is this the only way to do it? How do other people do it? Are there short cuts or alternative ways of doing it?
- **Constraints**. What can you do that you think you *can't* do? Are you certain that you *must* do certain things? What could you do differently? What rules can you break? What constraints don't actually exist?

Loosening the structure of the problem like this will help you look at the problem in different ways and help you generate new solutions.

What to do

Well structured or ill structured?

Are these problems well structured or ill structured? In each case, think about how well you can define the problem's:

- initial conditions;
- goal conditions;
- operators; and
- restraints and constraints.

There's no single answer: it depends on how you see the problem. How do you decide on the structure of each problem? What will influence your view of the problem's structure in each case?

- You weigh 220 pounds and you want to weigh 165 pounds.
- What is the solution to the equation $2x + 5 = 17$?
- Your manager is unhappy with the report you have written on current market conditions.
- It's 12 noon on Thursday. You need to be in Paris by 5pm.
- Your company is currently operating seven different IT systems to manage its assembly and distribution networks. The CEO has asked you to lead a project to rationalize down to one system.
- You're a GP. A patient comes into your surgery complaining of vague pains in her stomach.
- The local council plans to stop cutting the grass verges on your street.
- How can we improve the take-up of benefits among minority communities?

The problem matrix

We now have two ways of analysing problems:

1. presented or constructed; and
2. well structured or ill structured.

If we combine these two criteria, we can create four types of problem.

I've given names to each of these four problem types. I call a well-structured presented problem a *puzzle*, and an ill-structured presented problem a *headache*. Well-structured constructed problems I call *plans*, and ill-structured constructed problems *dreams*.

We can visualize these four types of problem, and the relationships between them, by placing them in a grid: what I call the problem matrix.

	Presented	Constructed
Well structured	1 Puzzle	3 Plan
Ill structured	2 Headache	4 Dream

1. Puzzles (presented; well structured)

A puzzle is, typically, a deviation from a norm. There's a gap between what *is* and what *should be*.

As with all presented problems, we can express a puzzle as a statement of what's wrong. The objective in solving a puzzle is *to put something right*.

Puzzles are well structured. For a problem to qualify as a puzzle, the deviation from the norm must be measurable. Puzzles usually have one right answer.

Most puzzles either are, or can be seen as, technical: a fault in a machine, an interruption in the power supply, a piece of equipment that won't work properly. The classic problem-solving process – diagnose the cause of the problem, remove the cause, solve the problem – will work *only* for this type of problem.

Typical examples

All of these can be puzzles: mending a piece of equipment; reconciling a set of accounts; making a process more efficient; improving productivity or personal performance in a measurable way.

What style to use?

 Solving a puzzle would typically involve using the skills of the Analyst and Engineer styles.

2 Headaches (presented; ill structured)

A headache, like a puzzle, is a deviation from the norm. We can express a headache as a statement of what's wrong; we can see a gap between *what is* and *what should be*. The aim in solving a headache is *to put something right*.

Unlike a puzzle, however, a headache is ill structured. We might identify a number of reasons for this lack of clarity:

- **Initial conditions**. We may not be able to identify a single cause of the fault, or to map the problem sufficiently accurately.

- **Goal conditions**. We may not be able to determine when the problem has been definitively solved. It may be unclear whether the problem has been solved once we have implemented a solution.

- **Operators**. We may not know how to reach the goal from our current situation; the problem may be unprecedented, so that we have no experience to draw on. Perhaps all past attempts to solve the problem have failed. Most irritatingly, seeking to solve a headache may actually intensify it – or transfer the pain somewhere else.

- **Constraints**. It may not be clear what we're allowed to do, or are forbidden from doing.

Much traditional problem-solving, especially in the corporate arena, spends a lot of time and effort trying to 'tame' headaches – typically, by transforming them into puzzles. Taming can be a legitimate strategy. Unfortunately, headaches often have a habit of recurring – sometimes in different places (or in different heads).

Some headaches are 'wicked' problems. Wicked problems – as we'll see in Chapter 7 – have specific characteristics. We may be able to deal with a wicked problem by taming it; and we may need to transform it into another type of problem: a plan or a dream. The problem will change radically if we do so – but perhaps that's what needs to happen to make any progress.

Typical examples

Headaches are nearly always problems involving a human element. In particular, we might identify a headache as a problem involving a group of stakeholders: individuals or groups who contribute to the problem by defining it differently, and who must also be involved in any solution.

A headache can be relatively small-scale. A persistently troublesome relationship at work, for example, or a personal relationship that's 'on the rocks', could both qualify as headaches. The problem could involve large numbers of people: problems with legacy IT systems – involving suppliers, users, budget-holders and even customers – are among the most common headaches currently afflicting large organizations. A headache may arise in relationships between organizations: industrial disputes and unhappy commercial contracts are usually headaches. And major social issues are often headaches: developing or preserving a local neighbourhood; reducing poverty in a city or community; achieving peace in a war zone.

What style to use?

Treating headaches nearly always requires an imaginative combination of thinking styles:

Making sense of a headache may seem to need all the skills of the Analyst style. But one of the defining features of a headache is that it cannot be entirely explained using rational methods; we may find ourselves succumbing to analysis paralysis in our efforts to understand the problem in detail.

We might turn to the Explorer style to gather more information about the problem, or to look for similar problems in different areas. Finding analogies may be a key to finding a way forward.

The Engineer style may help in breaking the problem down into manageable parts and fixing what can be fixed.

But the Designer style may well be crucial in creating a solution that is new and acceptable to all stakeholders.

3 Plans (constructed; well structured)

Plans are examples of constructed problems. We can express a plan as a phrase beginning with the words 'how to'. A plan is a problem we set ourselves: we might call it a challenge or an ambition. Our objective in solving a plan is *to create something new.*

Plans are well structured. We see a measurable gap between what *is* and what *could be*; we can define or measure our progress towards the goal and the goal itself. We map out plans in terms of *objectives, targets, milestones* and *measures of success*. Any well-managed project is an example of a plan.

Typical examples

Think of these as typical plans: gaining a qualification; giving up smoking; working out objectives after an appraisal; setting a budget; building a new sports complex.

What style to use?

As with puzzles, the Analyst and Engineer styles will usually be predominant in constructing plans. All the tools and techniques of project management seek to exploit these rational styles to the full.

But the Explorer style always helps us look at aspects of the problem in new ways; and the Designer style can also be brought in to help deliver more elegant, efficient plans of action.

4 Dreams (constructed; ill structured)

A dream, like a plan, is a constructed problem. We can express it as a 'how to' statement. Like a plan, a dream is a problem we set ourselves: a challenge or an ambition. Our aim is *to create something new.*

Unlike a plan, however, a dream's objective is unclear. Or rather, it's only broadly clear what we want to achieve. We're not at the point where we can set up a project to achieve our goal; rather, we have a rough notion of what we would like to achieve.

Typical examples

Dreams might include: finding a new career; innovating a new product; transforming the way we make or do something; making our school more welcoming; increasing customer satisfaction.

What style to use?

Tackling dreams begins with understanding the potential in a situation: the Explorer style will predominate over the Analyst style. Making something new always draws on the skills of the Designer style.

But making our dreams into feasible, workable solutions usually demands a healthy dose of Analyst and Engineer. The danger is that we turn to these styles of rational thinking too soon, before we've explored the available options.

Using the problem matrix

In the next four chapters, we'll look at each of these types of problem in more detail. We'll see what different skills, tools and techniques we can use to tackle each type of problem, and how each problem type generates a different type of solution.

Meanwhile, let's remind ourselves: the only difference between these four types of problem is in the way we look at them. We can *choose* to see a problem as being of a certain type. Our choice of solution – the action we take – depends on how we categorize the problem.

Just as we can choose how to look at a problem, we can choose to look at a problem *differently*. The problem matrix can help us to see how we're looking at a problem, and it can help us look at the problem in new ways. By moving a problem around the grid, we can *transform* a problem from one type to another. We might also split a problem into parts and solve each part differently.

What to do

Entering the matrix

Take a problem that currently interests or concerns you. Express the problem as *either* a statement of what's wrong, or as a 'how to'.

Decide whether the problem is well structured or ill structured by examining:

- initial conditions (where are you now?);
- goal conditions (where do you want to be?);
- operators (how can you move from initial to goal conditions?); and
- constraints (what limits your capacity to act?).

Based on this analysis, place the problem in one of the quadrants of the problem matrix.

Use Figure 5.1 to guide your thinking.

Now ask these three questions:

1 Where would you *like* to place the problem? You may be happy to see the problem remain in the quadrant of the problem matrix where you have placed it. You may want to look at the problem differently. If you had the choice (and you do!), how would you like to see the problem?

2 How would you need to change the problem in order to place it in your chosen quadrant?

3 What could you do to change the problem in the way you wish? The courses of action you identify are potential solutions – or pathways towards solutions.

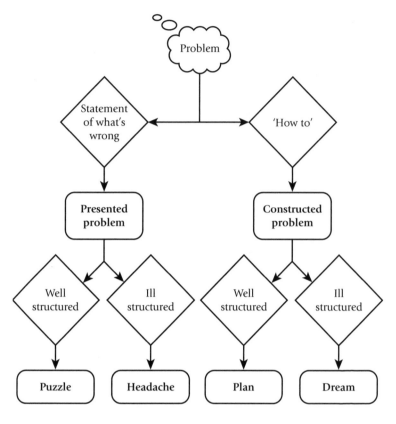

Figure 5.1 To guide your thinking

In brief

We can see problems as **presented** or **constructed**.

We can express a presented problem as **a statement of what's wrong**.

We can express a constructed problem as **a phrase beginning with the words 'how to'**.

We can define a problem's **structure** by looking at four key elements:

- initial conditions (where we are);
- goal conditions (where we want to be);
- operators (the different ways in which we can get from initial conditions to goal conditions); and
- constraints (whatever limits our action).

Well-structured problems are clear in all respects. Ill-structured problems are unclear in one or more respects.

- **Puzzles** are well-structured presented problems.
- **Headaches** are ill-structured presented problems.
- **Plans** are well-structured constructed problems.
- **Dreams** are ill-structured constructed problems.

We can use the **problem matrix** to understand a problem more clearly, and to transform our perception of a problem so that we can approach it differently.

Chapter

6

Closing the gap: solving puzzles

"The other day, I decided to cycle into town. When I looked at the bicycle, I noticed that one of the tyres was flat. Problem! A quick visual inspection showed nothing obviously wrong: no nails or pieces of glass puncturing the tyre. I took a chance, pumped up the tyre, noticed that it inflated and seemed to stay that way, and cycled successfully into town and back.

The next morning, I checked the tyre again. It was definitely softer than the day before, but not completely flat. A slow puncture, evidently. Only two probable causes: a hole in the inner tube or a leaky valve. I removed the tyre, extracted the inner tube, inflated it a little more and submerged it bit by bit in a bowl of water. In a few seconds the cause of the problem was clear: the seal around the valve had worn and was leaking a tiny stream of bubbles. So now I faced a simple decision: repair or replace? I could try patching, but the area around the valve would be awkward to mend effectively. Time to use the spare inner tube on the shelf!"

The slow puncture is a classic example of a puzzle. The problem presented itself to me. (I certainly didn't want a flat tyre that morning.) There was a measurable gap between what should be (the tyre should be permanently inflated) and what was (it was slowly deflating). The problem was very well structured: initial conditions and goal conditions were both precise (although I needed time to discern the goal conditions).

There was only one possible cause of the gap (air was leaking from the tube). The operator was clear: I had to find the location of the leak. Constraints were clear: I couldn't damage the inner tube any further, and I had to work with the inner tube I had. A touch of experience and expertise helped.

A quick note

For each type of problem, I'll give you a key features box like the one below as a quick reference. For every problem, I'll also give you one or more heuristics. A heuristic is a method of solving a problem that's reasonable because it's based on experience. The word comes from the Greek verb Εὑρίσκω, meaning 'to find' – the same word that gives us 'Eureka!' (which means 'I've found it!'). Think of a heuristic as being halfway between a hunch and a mathematical formula. (You'll find more about heuristics in Chapter 10.)

Puzzles: key features

- Problem definition: a statement of what's wrong.
- There is a gap between what *is* and what *should be*.
- The gap is measurable.
- There is usually only one right answer.
- Solution: close the gap.
- Leading heuristics: root cause analysis; repair; replace.

Recognizing a puzzle

A puzzle is a well-structured presented problem. There's a gap between what *is* and what *should be*. The gap is measurable (if we can't measure the gap, then the problem becomes ill structured and therefore not a puzzle). Solving the problem means closing the gap. And closing the gap usually means finding the *cause* of the gap. The solution to a puzzle is nearly always either to repair or to replace what causes the gap (see Figure 6.1).

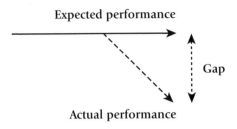

Figure 6.1 The solution to a puzzle

Puzzles usually have single, correct solutions, which we can arrive at systematically. The puzzles in puzzle books or in the newspaper, the problems set for mathematics homework, a chess problem – all are carefully structured problems that can be solved by using some kind of clear protocol, either simple or (as with chess) complicated.

Puzzles in real life are often technical problems – things going wrong or not performing as we expect them to: the car doesn't start; the computer has crashed (again); we should be processing 70 units an hour and we are processing only 45.

We can regard a problem as a puzzle even if it doesn't affect a machine or a technical system. Medical diagnosis often involves identifying a deviation from a normal level of performance: the pulse should be 60 and is running at 130; blood pressure should be 120:80 and is reading 150:110. We can regard managerial performance problems as puzzles: a saleswoman should be bringing in fifteen new clients a month and she is only achieving eight; a manager should be meeting his budget and is consistently overshooting.

Seeing a problem as a puzzle, however, will dehumanize the problem. Even if we're looking at human activity, focusing on a measurable gap between actual and required performance means that we will be inclined to view a puzzle in terms of a system or process.

Solving puzzles: what styles work best?

 Puzzles lend themselves principally to the Analyst and Engineer styles of problem-solving. That's because puzzles are problems where something in the present is wrong and needs to be put right. Analyst helps us to find the fault; Engineer helps us to correct the fault. That doesn't mean that Explorer and Designer are unwelcome when we're solving puzzles, but Analyst and Engineer take the lead.

We need two things to solve a puzzle: experience and expertise. We need experience to recognize where the gap is, and expertise to measure it. We need both to identify and deal with the cause of the gap.

Viewing a problem as a puzzle has definite advantages:

- **One problem at a time.** For a start, viewing a problem as a puzzle simplifies complexity. Rather than being overwhelmed by a mass of presented problems, we can focus on one variable, isolate what's wrong and put it right. This step-by-step approach can help us achieve real progress in difficult situations.

- **Elimination of superstitious thinking.** Clarifying the structure of a problem makes it less likely that we'll construct irrelevant explanations and useless solutions for the problem. If we can identify the precise cause of a pain, we can take steps to remove or correct the cause and bring ourselves back to health. Without the protocol of a rational medical intervention, we might resort to all sorts of useless quackery.

- **Reduction of blame.** Tackling a problem as a puzzle separates the problem from the person presenting it. We can concentrate on the measurable gap in performance without engaging in personal, subjective criticism.

Finding the root cause: the total quality approach

The idea that solving a problem essentially means finding what caused it has become hugely influential in organizational life. It's most closely associated with the concept of total quality management (TQM).

TQM starts from the proposition that, in industrialized societies, we form organizations to get work done. Those organizations are principally industrial – converting raw materials or parts into physical products; or bureaucratic – converting knowledge and expertise into new, useable knowledge or action.

As work becomes more complicated, so do our organizations and the networks between them. We need complex systems and processes to manage them. However, our organizations aren't machines; they are run by people. And people make mistakes, often and frequently. We create imperfect systems and processes, and we manage them imperfectly. So we need to monitor and manage the processes and systems in our organizations – continuously.

Root cause analysis is a typical TQM tool. It's based on the recognition that problems will arise in processes and systems operated by human beings. Its guiding philosophy is that root causes exist, that they can be identified by careful investigation and analysis and that correcting root causes is the best way to prevent similar problems from recurring in the future.

Root cause analysis comes in different forms. Nearly all of these forms start from a basic, three-part definition of a root cause. (I've given an example of each element from my tyre-repair example.)

- It must allow us to *demonstrate* a cause-and-effect linkage to the problem we're investigating. (I can demonstrate that the air is coming from a leaky valve.)

- It must be *controllable*. In other words, the cause of the problem must be as much within our circle of influence as the initial problem. (I may not be able to repair the valve, but I can replace the inner tube.)

- It must be *measurably correctable*. We must be able to remove, repair or replace the cause of the problem in such a way that we can observe or measure the effects of removing, repairing or replacing it. (I can measure the tyre pressure over time to check that the repair has worked.)

Asking 'Why?' five times

Among the simpler and most popular of these methods is the 'five whys'. The technique was originally developed by Sakichi Toyoda, and was later used by Toyota when developing its manufacturing processes. The tool is now used and promoted extensively, both within industry and beyond. If you have ever had anything to do with *kaizen* or Six Sigma, you'll have come across the five whys.

Here's a typical example of the technique tackling a simple technical problem.

Problem statement: *The car won't start.*

1. *Why?* The battery is dead.
2. *Why?* The alternator is not working.
3. *Why?* The alternator belt has broken.
4. *Why?* The alternator belt had reached the end of its recommended life and we hadn't replaced it.
5. *Why?* We have not been using the company service manual to maintain the car.
6. *Why?* Replacement parts are not available because of the extreme age of the vehicle.

Note that this list actually contains six 'Why' statements. The number 5 in the name of this technique is not critically important. In fact in this instance both of the final 'Why?' statements offer potential solutions:

- Start using the company service manual to look after the car.
- Find a specialist supplier of replacement parts for elderly cars.

An important point about root cause statements: they must be specific, and must refer either to a process or to a behaviour that can be managed. Generalized statements such as 'there's not enough time', 'we lack resources' or 'because management doesn't like doing it that way', can't be allowed as root cause statements. However true such statements may be, they violate one or more of the three defining features of a root cause: we may not be able to demonstrate a link between the cause and the problem; the cause may be out of our control; and it may not be measurably correctable (how could we measure 'sufficient time' or 'enough resources'?).

The key is to concentrate on processes rather than people. Any cause statement that involves blaming a person or group of people is missing the point. If in doubt, always check that you are asking a version of the question: 'Why did the process fail?'.

To keep yourself on track, ask these questions every time you answer the question 'Why?':

- Is there any proof of this statement: something you can measure or observe?
- Is there any evidence that this root cause has actually produced the problem in the past?
- Is there anything behind or beyond the stated cause that might be a more probable cause?
- What does this stated cause need in order to cause the problem?
- Are there any other causes that could produce the problem?

What to do

Asking five whys: critique

Here is a 'five why' analysis from a health service website. Can you see where the analysis becomes weak and could be improved?

Problem statement: *The patient's diagnosis of skin cancer was considerably delayed.*

1 *Why?* The surgeon had not seen the excision biopsy report.

2 *Why?* The report was filed in the patient's notes without being seen by the surgeon.

3 *Why?* It was the receptionist's job to do the filing.

4 *Why?* The junior doctors were busy with other tasks.

5 *Why?* The junior doctors' other tasks were seen as more important than filing.

The five whys technique is undoubtedly useful for tackling relatively simple puzzles. However, the more complicated the problem, the more likely it is that asking 'Why?' will take you down multiple trails that may only serve to confuse you further. Other potential problems with the technique are that:

- you might stop at a symptom and seek to solve that, rather than pressing on to the root cause;
- you are limited by your current knowledge: you can't find causes that you don't already know about (hence the need to support the technique with extensive investigation and information-gathering);
- you may be hampered by lack of managerial support to help you ask the really important 'Why' questions; and
- it may not be objective; different groups may well find different causes for the same problem.

I suspect that the five whys technique has become famous for reasons other than its usefulness as a problem-solving tool. It seems to chime with a basic human need for patterns of causality. We all know how much children love asking the question 'Why?' repeatedly, almost as a kind of ritual. There's something intuitively satisfying about a causal sequence that starts with something small and extends to an unexpected or catastrophic consequence.

An old proverbial rhyme exploits this fascination with unforeseen consequences:

For want of a nail

For want of a nail the shoe was lost.
For want of a shoe the horse was lost.
For want of a horse the rider was lost.
For want of a rider the battle was lost.
For want of a battle the kingdom was lost.
And all for the want of a horseshoe nail.

Kepner-Tregoe: solving puzzles the rational way

One of the best known approaches to puzzles is the Kepner-Tregoe (K-T) problem-solving approach. Charles Kepner and Benjamin Tregoe developed their ideas in the 1950s and published *The Rational Manager* in 1965. Since founding their company, Kepner-Tregoe, in 1958, these two consultants have developed their tools and techniques into a formidable body of knowledge and practice.

The K-T approach is based on the fundamental principle that the best way to solve a performance problem is to reduce it to the parameters of a puzzle. In that respect, it shares features with many other problem-solving techniques developed to improve productivity in industry – mainly in manufacturing.

K-T starts with a very simple definition of a problem:

- Do we have a deviation?
- Is the cause unknown?
- Do we need to know the cause to take effective action?

If the answer to all three questions is 'Yes', we have a problem.

For Kepner and Tregoe, the way we describe the problem is critically important. All our analysis to find the cause of the problem, and to repair or replace it, derives from the way we state the problem. And a good way to check whether we are starting in the right place with our problem description is to ask whether we know the cause of the deviation we are investigating. The key question is:

"Can we explain the effect of this problem, as we have described it?"

If the answer is 'yes', then we need to back up to the point where we can no longer explain the cause of the deviation.

For example, if the problem statement is, 'Coolant on the ground under the engine after several hours' standing', we can explain the cause with no difficulty: 'Coolant is leaking from the engine'. There isn't any other rational explanation for the presence of the coolant on the ground, so we need to redefine the problem: 'Coolant is leaking from the engine'.

Kepner and Tregoe also point out that the problem statement must be specific, not vague or generalized. 'Low productivity on the assembly line' or 'poor performance in the claims section' are inadequate as problem statements. We need to name *one* object, or kind of object, or system; and *one* malfunction, *one* deviation, whose cause we're investigating.

And then we need to be able to show the evidence for the deviation: either in simple sensory terms, or by measuring something. For example, we can certainly see the coolant lying on the ground, and we could measure the levels of coolant in the engine. As Kepner and Tregoe write:

"We must describe exactly what we see, feel, hear, smell, or taste that tells us there is a deviation.**"**

K-T proceeds by asking us to state what the problem is *not*. For example, sales may be dropping in one branch of a retail chain, but not in another; parts may fail when fitted to one machine, but not when fitted to others.

The next crucial stage in this analysis is to identify *possible causes* of the problem. How *could* the deviation be caused? By including all possible causes, we maintain our objectivity about the problem and reduce the potential for disagreement or blame. We're looking for the root cause of a problem, the true cause. And the true cause must explain each and every effect that we have observed or measured.

Indeed, the final stages of this process include *testing* possible causes against the problem definition, until one or more causes are confirmed as the root cause. The overall aim of the exercise is to demonstrate a clear, unequivocal cause-and-effect relationship so that we know which cause to repair or replace.

Kepner and Tregoe are realistic about the limitations of such a systematic approach to problem analysis. The process helps people work together to pool information and think rationally about it. But, in a modern industrial or bureaucratic environment, many problems are so complex that they may not have a single root cause. They write:

"If we cannot track down the key facts needed to crack a problem, that problem will continue to defy solution. No approach or process, however systematically or meticulously applied, will unlock its secret."

In other words, some presented problems are irreducible to the clear structure of a puzzle. In the next chapter we'll look at the considerable challenges that result, and how we can go about meeting them.

In brief

Puzzles: key features

- Problem definition: a statement of what's wrong.
- There is a gap between what *is* and what *should be*.
- The gap is measurable.
- Usually one right answer.
- Solution: close the gap.
- Leading heuristics: root cause analysis; repair; replace.

Solving a puzzle means closing the gap between what is and what should be. Closing the gap usually means finding the *cause* of the gap. The solution to a puzzle is nearly always either to repair or to replace what causes the gap.

Puzzles tend to have single, correct solutions. They tend to be technical problems. We can regard a problem as a puzzle, even if it doesn't affect a machine or a technical system. Seeing a problem as a puzzle, however, tends to dehumanize the problem.

Puzzles lend themselves principally to the Analyst and Engineer styles of problem-solving.

We need two things to solve a puzzle: experience and expertise.

Viewing a problem as a puzzle has definite advantages.

- **one problem at a time**;
- **elimination of superstitious thinking**;
- **reduction of blame**.

The idea that solving a problem essentially means finding what caused it has become hugely influential in organizational life. Root cause analysis is a typical tool, and comes in different forms. Among the simplest and most popular is the 'five whys' technique.

One of the best known approaches to puzzles is the Kepner-Tregoe problem-solving approach. K-T starts with a *specific problem statement*. It proceeds by identifying *possible causes* of the problem. The final stages of this process include *testing* possible causes against the problem definition,

The K-T approach is based on the assumption that the best way to solve a performance problem is to reduce it to the parameters of a puzzle. However, Kepner and Tregoe are realistic about the limitations of such a systematic approach to problem analysis. Not every presented problem is reducible to the clear structure of a puzzle.

Chapter

7

Treating headaches: what to do when problems become wicked

In 2003, the UK government instigated the National Programme for IT, a scheme designed to link over 30,000 GPs and 300 hospitals in the country. The project was budgeted at £6 billion and was to include, among other things, an online booking system, a centralized medical records system for 50 million patients, e-prescriptions and fast computer network links between NHS organizations. By 2006, two years into the project's 10-year lifespan, a group of academics was calling for an independent review. A journalist at the time wrote:

> "Technology is still seen as just another form of engineering. But IT systems are not like bridges – they are a tool, not an entity. ... Technology is a process, with no clear start, no clear end and ever-shifting goalposts. And as fast as IT itself evolves, the potential uses of it morph and multiply. There is no end date. The bridge is never built. But that does not mean it is a disaster. That is simply how it should be."
>
> computing.co.uk, 27 April 2006

By 2011, the project budget had ballooned to over £11 billion and a new government announced that it would be dismantled. The announcement, however, was more a PR exercise than an accurate description of what was happening. The programme's architecture had changed; what initially had been conceived as an enormous top-down project was now a patchwork of different programmes, generated locally and then plugged together.

When a presented problem becomes ill structured, it ceases to be a puzzle. The vagueness or complexity of the problem causes stress. Hence the name I give to such problems: *headaches*.

Headaches: key features

- Problem definition: a statement of what's wrong.
- Gap: between what *is* and what *should be*.
- The problem statement is ill defined: initial conditions, goal conditions, operators, restraints or constraints unclear.

Key heuristics: transform the problem into a puzzle, plan or dream.

A problem may be a headache for various reasons. We might lack the expertise to solve it: I can mend a puncture but I can't change the clutch on my car. We might have been presented with a problem but not given clear goal conditions: how can your friendly IT consultant rebuild your network if you're not sure how you want it to operate? We may not be able to judge a solution's effectiveness without implementing it – by which time it may be too late ('I think this improvised rope bridge will bear our weight; shall we try it out?'). And we may be overwhelmed by the sheer complexity of the problem: how do we manage climate change, or mediate between warring communities in a disputed territory?

Solving headaches: what styles work best?

Headaches lend themselves, at least to begin with, to the Explorer style. Headaches, by definition, are unsolvable; in order to tackle them, we need to *transform* them into another kind of problem. Explorer helps us find different ways of seeing the problem, giving us new possibilities of dealing with it. We shall probably need the other styles at some point, but Explorer is vital at the early stages.

In this chapter, we'll look at the treatment options for head-aches, in increasing order of effectiveness:

- Treat the presenting symptom.
- Deny that the headache exists.
- Transform the headache into a puzzle.
- Model the problem system.
- Recognize the problem as wicked.

Treat the presenting symptom

The first option is to act immediately to stop the pain. Take a pill; put a sticking plaster on the wound; shore up the collaps-ing wall; throw money into the gaping financial hole.

Obviously, treating the symptom may stave off disaster for a while, and it may relax the stress. No bad thing. But none of these solutions is likely to be lasting or satisfactory. Taking emergency action may give you thinking time; but you need to use that time wisely to find a better course of action.

In particular, don't take emergency action and then …

Deny that the headache exists

… which is, of course, what we do, all too often.

The obvious sign of denial is that we give up looking for a solution. We might distract ourselves with other activities. At work, we might just follow orders, do our job, and try not to get in trouble. Maybe the organization will fix the problem at a higher level, in a new version, or at the latest restructuring.

Another common symptom of denial is to assert that the problem is already solved. It's much easier to do this if you fail to specify the problem clearly. An addict may claim that he doesn't have a drink problem, because it might be hard to define the point at which alcohol addiction kicks in. A poli-tician may claim that her policy has reduced the number of patients waiting for serious operations, by carefully failing to define the word 'serious'.

Denial is an abnegation of responsibility. We are moving the problem out of our circle of influence into our circle of concern. We may then find ourselves engaging in the two behaviours typical of problems that sit in our circle of concern: blame or resistance (look back at Chapter 4 for more on these responses).

Sometimes it may be a very good idea to give up responsibility for a headache – or to give up some responsibility. This isn't denial – it's managing our responsibility productively.

What to do

Learning to say 'No'

Giving up responsibility for a headache is not in itself a bad thing to do. There is no shame in admitting that you are overwhelmed by a problem. The key to dealing with a headache is to *manage* your responsibility.

You have two options:

1 Hand the problem over to someone else.

2 Share the problem.

Learning to say 'No' is a vital part of your problem-solving skill set.

Alternatively, seek support. Talk the problem over with someone you trust. Use some of the techniques in this chapter to analyse the problem, break it down into parts and share out responsibilities.

A problem shared really can be a problem halved.

If you decide you want to retain responsibility for a headache, you need to *transform* it because, as a headache, it's almost certainly unsolvable. We can use the problem matrix to find ways of transforming the problem.

	Presented	Constructed
Well structured	1 Puzzle	3 Plan
Ill structured	2 Headache	4 Dream

The alternative to treating the presenting symptom, or denying that the problem exists, is to *transform* the headache into a different type of problem.

Transform the headache into a puzzle

The aim here is to tame the problem: to reduce and simplify it to manageable proportions. And to do that, we need to improve the problem's *structure*.

The aim of the transformation is to increase the clarity of the problem's:

- initial conditions,
- goal conditions,
- operators,
- constraints.

One of the easiest ways to transform a headache into a puzzle is to look for an expert to help you. Solving puzzles, as we've seen, requires **expertise** and **experience**. Indeed, we employ experts – plumbers, electricians, financial advisers, IT consultants – precisely in order to turn our headaches into neat puzzles.

We can learn from the experts:

- **Experts codify the problem-solving process.** They use manuals, tried-and-tested procedures or regulated protocols. They pass examinations to show that they understand them.

- **Experts concentrate on clarifying initial and goal conditions.** They'll work hard to define the problem state and the goal state as clearly as possible.

- **Experts establish measures of success.** They know that the solution to a puzzle must be testable. Often, they'll test by measuring, and use a mechanical device to ensure that the measurement is objective and accurate.

- **Experts can test a solution without risking catastrophe.** Whether it's checking that the aircraft is airworthy or testing a disaster-recovery system, experts design procedures that will test whether their solution is robust without endangering the system itself.

If we can do the same with some of our own headaches, we can successfully transform them into puzzles. We can become our own experts.

How to transform a headache into a puzzle

If you want to try transforming a headache into a puzzle yourself, try the following.

1. **Tighten the problem definition.** Limit the problem to a local, measurable set of variables. For example, if you're trying to clean up a database, limit the number of variables by which you can cross-link items. If you want to reduce violence in a school, focus on measurable sub-problems: stop students carrying knives by installing metal detectors; monitor the number of physical assaults on teachers and look for ways to reduce them; record lessons and count the number of verbal assaults. Resist at all costs any tendency to let the problem definition expand or become vague.

2. **Define a clear 'stopping point'.** How will you know that the problem is solved? Can you run a test that will demonstrate that your database is now complete, with no errors or repetitions? Will you stop your anti-violence campaign when assaults of teachers have been reduced to zero?

3. **Limit the number of solutions.** One way to limit the number of solutions is to set yourself a clear limit: for example, that you will consider only three or four. One of the most dramatic limits is to look for two opposing solutions: an 'either/or' choice that clarifies your thinking and can spur you to action. For example, you could tell yourself that *either* you will manage your diet more effectively, *or* you will put yourself at risk of contracting type 2 diabetes within five years.

4. **Specify how you intend to measure success.** With a limited number of variables to cross-link items in a database, you can check whether the database is performing to spec. If you count the number of knives brought into the school, and it goes down to zero, you can say that you have solved the problem.

5. **Redefine the problem so that it resembles a previous, solved problem.** Filter out, or ignore, information that complicates the picture. 'It's just like that problem. This solution worked then; it should work now.' The success of the previous solution may convince you that it will work in this instance.

Turning a headache into a puzzle has many advantages. It brings the problem within your circle of influence, giving you a sense of control and the opportunity to use puzzle-solving tools and techniques. And that reduces stress. The satisfaction of seeing success materialize before your eyes will increase your sense of competence, giving you the courage to tackle further problems. Use this strategy to break down complex problems into manageable parts, or to extract puzzle elements from larger, intractable problems.

What to do

Ishikawa analysis: finding causes of headaches

Ishikawa (or fishbone) diagrams develop cause and effect analysis. In situations where the causes of a problem cannot be easily measured, or where the issue is complex, Ishikawa diagrams help to clarify the major issues and the links between causes:

▶

1 State the problem: a simple sentence in a box on the right-hand side of a piece of flipchart paper.

2 Draw a horizontal line across the page, to the left of the problem box.

3 Ask: 'Why is the problem occurring?' Place each cause on a line running at 45 degrees from the main stem.

4 For each cause, add sub-causes to the appropriate 'rib'.

The main ribs will probably take on more general headings. You might, for example, decide to use these headings as the main ribs of your diagram:

- manpower, methods, materials and machinery (recommended for manufacturing);

- equipment, policies, procedures and people (recommended for administration and service).

The basic layout of an Ishikawa diagram is shown in Figure 7.1 .

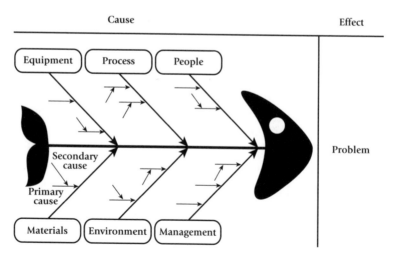

Figure 7.1 An Ishikawa diagram

Some huge problems are puzzles that may have headaches embodied in them. In 1961, John F. Kennedy set his nation a very well-structured problem: to put a man on the surface of the Moon and return him safely to Earth. Solving the problem involved large numbers of headaches, some with tragic consequences; but the main problem was clearly defined, with a limited number of solutions and clear measures of success.

The risks of taming a headache

Taming a headache carries some risks. Here are the most important.

A puzzle can still be hard to solve. Taming a headache may bring the problem under our control, but we shouldn't assume that the resulting problem will be simple. Calculating the square root of 5734, finding the shortest route to a given destination, decommissioning a nuclear reactor – all of these are puzzles, but they have varying degrees of difficulty. The point about all three, however, is that, with the appropriate expertise and experience, almost anybody could solve them.

Limiting the problem definition may simply shift the problem. We may think we're simplifying the problem, but we may be doing no more than allowing the real problem to scurry away and raise its head somewhere else. Trying to make our organization more efficient by, for example, reducing the number of staff, might simply transfer inefficiencies to new external suppliers, temporary staff or contractors.

Measurement can be a double-edged sword. 'What gets measured gets done': we often use that quotation, both to justify measuring and monitoring, and to criticize them. Metrics may give us objective indications that a solution is working; and they may tell us simply that something is being measured. We measure academic performance in schools principally by monitoring pass rates in examinations, but what do such measures tell us about the quality of teaching or learning? We measure many aspects of performance in our hospitals, but how much do such measures indicate that healthcare is improving – or that we are becoming healthier?

Albert Einstein reportedly had a sign on his office wall: 'Not everything that counts can be counted, and not everything that can be counted counts.' The aim of problem-solving is to change a situation for the better. And measurement alone can never do that.

The headache may not be like previous problems. Viewing a problem as a repeat of a past problem may be helpful, but if the problem is truly complex it will probably be more *unlike* previous problems than like them. Using past, successful solutions might then become counter-productive, or even damaging.

Model the problem system

Problem-modelling takes us a stage further in the task of transforming headaches into puzzles. The aim of modelling is to represent the *system* within which a headache arises. We can then discover *points of intervention*: places in the system where we can act to solve the problem.

So what's a system?

A system, according to Simon Baron-Cohen in his book *The Essential Difference*, is 'anything which is governed by rules specifying input-operation-output relationships'.

Obvious examples of systems are technical for example: watches, central heating systems, or aircraft. A musical instrument becomes a system in conjunction with the person playing it. A house might be seen as a system; so might a town or a shopping precinct. We can see libraries, companies, board games, ponds, yachts or gardens as systems. A system might be small (a cell in an organism) or very large (a social group or an economic system).

The most important point about systems is that they are well structured. Identify the rules governing the system and you can predict its workings precisely.

For example, if I flick the switch in my living room, the light comes on. The switch is the input, my flicking it is the operation, and the light illuminating is the output.

Identify the variables in the system

To analyse a system, we first identify the variables in the system. We then observe what happens when each of those variables shifts. By repeated and close observation, we can work out the rules that govern the behaviour of the system: from input, through operation, to output.

For example, a central heating system will include variables such as the pressure of the fluid in the system, the amount of fuel heating the fluid, the number of radiators built into the system, and so on.

Modelling the system

To understand a system more easily, it helps to model it. The simplest models of problems are graphic – pictures or diagrams drawn on paper or a whiteboard:

- A flowchart models a process, from input through operation to output.
- A map models a piece of terrain.
- A tree chart might model an organizational structure or a set of decisions and their consequences.

Models can be three-dimensional: we can represent the problem of reducing fuel consumption in a vehicle, for example, by making a model of the vehicle and placing it in a wind tunnel, to study its aerodynamic performance. Models can also be mathematical or coded in computer language.

All models simplify complex situations; good models simplify usefully.

A good model adheres to the following rules:

- **The model must be transparent.** We must be able to inspect and understand the rules and principles the model is using.
- **The model must be testable.** It must work to inputs that we can define and determine, and it must yield outputs we can observe and measure.

The critical question when modelling a problem is to decide what *kind* of problem we want to model. The model of the problem will derive from the type of problem we choose: how we label it. If we label the problem 'a manufacturing problem', we will generate a model showing the flow of materials and information, the processes and controls used, evaluation of output quality, and so on. A financial problem might involve variables from the income statement, balance sheet or chart of accounts (sales, expenses, costs, assets, long-term and short-term debt, and so on).

The model we use depends on how we classify the problem.

Identifying the desired outputs

Once we've modelled the system, we can begin to ask what *outputs* we're looking for. For example, if we turn up the central heating, the increase in heat emitted is the output.

The key with outputs is to identify how the existing outputs differ from our desired outputs. (A presented problem, you'll recall, involves a gap between what *is* and what *should be*.) Existing outputs can differ from desired outputs in four ways:

1. What do you want to *achieve*? (What do you want that you don't have?)

2. What do you want to *preserve*? (What do you have that you want to keep?)

3. What do you want to *avoid*? (What don't you want to have?)

4. What do you want to *eliminate*? (What do you have that you don't want?)

And, this being a system, we're looking for outputs that are measurable. Only by measuring them can we see whether the output has changed in the way we want. (The model shown in Figure 7.2 derives from the work of Fred Nickols.)

		Do you want it?	
		Yes	*No*
Do you have it?	*No*	Achieve	Avoid
	Yes	Preserve	Eliminate

Figure 7.2 Measurable outputs

Identifying the points of intervention and evaluation

The only way to change existing outputs into desired outputs is to *intervene* in the system. And because we want to know whether our intervention has been successful, we also need to identify the point where we can *evaluate* our intervention. Because we're working with a system, change will be indirect: we'll almost certainly have to intervene at one point in the system in order to change the outputs at a different point.

Think back to our central heating system. We want to make the house warmer. The points of intervention to achieve that increase are the thermostatic control, the taps on the radiators and the central controls on the boiler. Of course, if we think of the *house* as a system, other points of intervention become important: the doors and windows, insulation layers in the roof, and so on. The point of evaluation is a thermometer – often incorporated into the thermostat.

If we've modelled the system well, we'll be able to create linkages between the *point of intervention* and the *point of evaluation*:

- With a simple system, we may be able to rely on a mental model: changing the fuse in the plug may result in the Christmas tree lights coming on, without the need to draw the system on a piece of paper.

- With more complex systems, a visual model becomes necessary. We need a set of drawings to help us assemble the flat-pack furniture, a circuit diagram to repair the hi-fi, or a map of a transport system to help us reach our destination.

Recognize the problem as wicked

Some headaches resist simplifying.

Consider these presented problems – all expressed as statements of what's wrong:

- The team doesn't work well together.
- Our road becomes dangerously congested when parents deliver or pick up their children from the local school.
- Our company has no clear strategy.
- We can't integrate customer preferences with product profiles in our current data management system.
- Our city is plagued by sectarianism that occasionally erupts into violence.
- The charity we work for is about to be merged with another charity with a very different management culture.
- The town centre fills with young people indulging in antisocial behaviour after the shops close.

There's a name for headaches of this kind. We call them *wicked*.

Wicked problems are the most ill structured of presented problems. They may have innumerable causes – or no identifiable cause. They're tough to define; and they can't be solved with a single course of action.

Simplifying a wicked problem into a puzzle may be counterproductive. You may find that your solution actually makes the problem worse by generating undesirable consequences. For example, managers may seek to improve a healthcare system by concentrating on a few measurable variables –

waiting times in surgeries or numbers of patients awaiting operations – both of which could have serious repercussions for quality of care.

Wicked problems resist modelling. Managers may find it hard to model the increasingly complex environment in which their organization operates. (How can we model customer preferences, for example?) As a result, they may be confronted with problems that they can't solve simply by gathering more data, analysing information or breaking a problem down into smaller, manageable problems.

Wicked problems have another defining characteristic: they involve people. Any problem involving a group of 'stakeholders' is likely to be wicked. The word 'stakeholder' is well chosen: when different people have a stake in a problem, they are likely to see the problem differently:

- **Initial conditions:** different people see the problem differently; they use different terms to define and describe the problem, even though they are all affected by it. Reaching agreement simply on what the problem is can be hugely difficult.

- **Goal conditions:** the people seeking to solve the problem may be different from the people who will be affected by the solution. Different people will demand different goals. Some may see the solution as another problem.

- **Operators:** different people will tackle the problem in different ways, especially if they are in different departments, different parts of a network, different professions or different cultures. Implementing a solution can become fraught with political peril.

- **Constraints:** different people will have different restrictions on their actions, different aims, priorities or values. They may also have conflicting ideas about what can or can't be done, and what must or must not be done.

The term 'wicked problem' was coined in the 1970s by Horst Rittel and Melvin M. Webber, professors of design and urban planning at the University of California in Berkeley. Since then, the term has been used principally for large-scale problems faced by corporations, nation states or the international community. But many small-scale problems are wicked: tensions within a family or a work team; conflict in a neighbourhood; growing a small business. It's not the size of the problem that makes it wicked, but its irreducible complexity.

The 10 characteristics of a wicked problem

As Rittel defined it, a wicked problem has 10 key characteristics:

1. **There is no single, definitive formulation of a wicked problem.** It's not possible to reduce the problem to a single statement of what is wrong.

2. **Every wicked problem can be considered a symptom of another problem.** A wicked problem is inextricably entwined with other problems – an evolving set of interlocking demands and constraints. Rittel said: 'One cannot understand the problem without knowing about its context.'

3. **Every discrepancy in a wicked problem can be explained in different ways.** If we were to ask all the stakeholders to do a 'five whys' analysis on a wicked problem, we would have completely different sequences of cause and effect.

4. **You don't understand the problem until you have developed a solution.** The structured two-stage process of problem-solving – understand the problem and generate a solution – will not work with a wicked problem. Rittel wrote: 'One cannot first understand, then solve.' Instead, we have to combine the two stages: try a solution; test it against the problem; adjust the solution and reapply; and so on. Solving the problem becomes part of the process of understanding the problem.

5. **Wicked problems have no stopping rule.** Since there's no single problem, there can be no single solution – only a solution that is provisionally good enough. Problem-solving will only end when we reach a solution that's good enough for the moment, or when we run out of resources: time, money or energy.

6. **Wicked problems do not have an exhaustive set of potential solutions.** There may be no solutions; there may be a host of potential solutions. We may be able to

generate a range of solutions, and we can be sure that there will be others that we will not think of. Which solutions are potentially valid? Which should we pursue? It's a matter of creativity and personal judgement.

7. **Solutions to wicked problems are not right or wrong.** They are simply better or worse; good enough or not good enough. We can't decide objectively whether the solution to a wicked problem is good or bad. We can evaluate solutions only in the social context of the stakeholders, all of whom are in some way competent to judge.

8. **Every wicked problem is unique.** Wicked problems include so many different factors, interlocking in such complex ways, that each problem is essentially novel. No two wicked problems are alike.

9. **Every solution to a wicked problem is a 'one-shot operation'.** We can't learn about a wicked problem without trying solutions, but because there is no opportunity to learn by trial and error, every attempt counts significantly. Solutions to puzzles can be easily tried and abandoned. Solutions to wicked problems are expensive and probably have expensive consequences – some of which may be irreversible. As Rittel said: 'One cannot build a freeway to see how it works.'

10. **The problem-solver has no right to be wrong.** Any action we take to solve a wicked problem will have wide-ranging consequences. If we are dealing with a wicked problem, we shall be held liable for the consequences of our actions. We can't avoid that responsibility.

First steps in tackling a wicked problem

Wicked problems can cause prolonged and painful stuckness. Whether the problem is personal or social, any solution to a wicked problem is likely to require radical and imaginative action to unstick our thinking. And, because a wicked problem involves a group of stakeholders, any solution is going to have to be collaborative.

Your aim must be to seek:

- shared understanding of the problem; and
- shared commitment to tackle it.

Seeking shared understanding of the problem

The first thing to do with a wicked problem is to discuss it. Bringing people together to discuss a complicated problem requires considerable skill. You'll need to manage the conversation and the group's thinking.

What to do

Establishing dialogue

Here are some initial guidelines to help you create genuine dialogue among the stakeholders of a wicked problem:

- **Ask for different perspectives.** Don't seek agreement too soon; take time to discover the views of different stakeholders. Discipline the conversation so that everyone has the opportunity to give their opinion. Forbid judgemental comments about any view.

- **Make the conversation public.** Don't be tempted to 'do deals' with individuals behind closed doors.

- **Focus on defining the problem, not solving it.** Work towards a definition of the problem that everyone can agree to.

- **Create a shared visual representation of the problem.** Draw a picture of the problem that everyone can refer to when discussing it. Using 'rich pictures' can be very useful here. (See Chapter 11 for more on this technique.)

- **Concentrate on possibility rather than probability.** Ask team members to imagine their ideal solutions; look for shared ambitions.

Building shared commitment

Commitment, as we saw in Chapter 4, is more than taking responsibility for a problem. Commitment is the highest level of problem ownership: at its most powerful, it generates a sense of unstoppable energy and concentration that we call the 'flow' state. How can we begin to generate 'flow' in a diverse group of stakeholders?

The problem matrix can help us. We've seen that one way to deal with a headache is to transform it into a puzzle. But two other transformations are possible: turning it into either a plan or a dream. To do either, you need to transform it from a presented problem into a constructed problem.

We saw earlier that presented problems and constructed problems are expressed differently. A presented problem is typically expressed as a statement of what's wrong. A constructed problem is typically expressed as a phrase beginning with the words 'how to'. The first move, then, in unsticking our thinking about a wicked problem is to express it as a constructed problem – as a 'how to'.

What to do

The power of 'how to'

Take a look at the problem definitions in the table below and transform each into a 'how to' statement, which you can write in the right-hand column.

Now find another 'how to' statement to express the same problem. And another. And another... For example, we could transform the first statement in the list into: *how to get our team to work better together.*

Further possible 'how to' statements might be;

- *how to improve team members' commitment to the team*;
- *how to provide better conditions for the team to work together*;
- *how to remove obstacles to effective teamwork*;

and so on. (You can undoubtedly think of yet another 'how to' statement to put in the box overleaf.)

What is happening to your thinking about the problem as you generate new 'how to' statements?

▶

The team doesn't work well together	
Our road becomes dangerously congested when parents drop off or collect their children from school	
Our company has no clear strategy	
We can't integrate customer preferences with product profiles in our data management system	
Our city is plagued by sectarianism that occasionally erupts into violence	
The charity we work for is about to be merged with another charity with a very different management culture	
At night the town centre fills with young people behaving anti-socially	

'How to' unsticks our thinking in some remarkable ways:

- First, we begin to think forwards into the future. Instead of thinking about what's wrong, we're asking what we might do.
- Second, instead of considering one intractable problem, we're considering multiple solutions.

We can use the 'how to' technique to involve different stake-holders in solving wicked problems. By focusing their minds on the future, on solutions and on multiple possibilities, the technique very quickly and simply focuses their minds on the issue at hand, dispelling blame and resistance and allowing different perspectives to be voiced.

The next chapter looks at the 'how to' technique in more detail. The first move remains the most important: to transform our perception of the problem so that it becomes either a plan or a dream – a constructed problem that we can feel committed to solving.

In brief

Headaches: key features

- Problem definition: a statement of what's wrong.
- Gap: between what *is* and what *should be*.
- The problem statement is ill defined: initial conditions, goal conditions, operators, restraints or constraints unclear.

We can tackle headaches in a number of ways, in increasing order of effectiveness:

- Treat the presenting symptom.
- Deny that the headache exists.
- Transform the headache into a puzzle.
- Model the problem system.
- Recognize the problem as wicked.

The first steps in approaching the problem as wicked are to create:

- shared understanding of the problem; and
- shared commitment to tackle it.

We create shared understanding through managed dialogue with stakeholders. We can begin to build shared commitment by phrasing the problem as a 'how to' – thus transforming it into a constructed problem.

Chapter

8

Design thinking: planning the way forward

Here's an exercise for you.

You'll need a blank piece of paper – at least A4 size would be good – and your wallet or purse. Put the blank piece of paper on the table and look at it. Go ahead: look at the paper for at least 15 seconds. It's blank. Let it be blank. There's nothing wrong with a blank piece of paper.

Now take everything out of your wallet or purse. Credit cards, photographs, old tickets or cash machine printouts, paper money and coins. You'll need at least 10 objects.

You're going to make a design on the blank piece of paper, using the objects from your wallet or purse. You can use only the objects you have, but you don't have to use all of them. You have three minutes. (Use a stopwatch or your wristwatch to measure the time; you're not allowed to go past the three-minute mark.)

Don't read on until you've completed the task.

Ready?

Go!

What you have just done is called design thinking.

I've just set you a constructed problem. Or rather: you have set *yourself* a constructed problem, because you've chosen to do the task.

Constructed problems: key characteristics

- We create them. They didn't exist until we thought of them. We are responsible for their existence.

- There is a perceived gap between what *is* and what *could be*.

- Solving them is *energizing*.

- They generate commitment – full ownership.

- Solving them can induce the flow state.

- Focus is on the solution and how to move towards it.

- Method: assembling available materials into workable solutions and checking them against ideal solutions.

Now let's think more about what it was like to solve this problem.

In this problem, there was nothing wrong: no fault to be put right, nothing to be repaired. (There's nothing wrong with a blank piece of paper.) And there was no right answer. You were interested in what *could* be, not what *should* be.

Were you happy with your design? Most people who do this exercise say that they are quite proud of what they've created. That's an important feature of constructed problems: we usually feel proud of the solutions we create, because we own them.

But if you're not particularly happy with your design, it's probably because you feel you could do better. You'd like to try again. That's also good: 'back to the drawing board' is another vital element of design thinking.

(You're allowed to stop at this point and have another go, if you want to. But stick to the rules: use only the objects you have, and take no more than three minutes. See you shortly.)

Now think about how you were feeling while you were completing the task.

Most people who do this exercise report that they felt energized, fully involved and focused on the task. The task 'took them out of themselves'. Time passed differently.

They felt *committed*.

If you felt like this, you were experiencing the flow state we explored in Chapter 4. The task helped you to find that state: it provided you with immediate feedback; the task was time-limited; and you were able to see the results at once. The task also nicely balanced challenge and skill: it was neither too easy nor too difficult, and in fact you were in control of the level of difficulty.

So much for your feelings. What about your actions? My guess is that you did one of two things:

1. Perhaps you stared at the paper for a short while and formed some kind of general design in your head. Then you began to use the objects at your disposal to move towards that 'ideal' design.

2. Or perhaps you started out by playing with the objects: moving them around, combining them in different ways and seeing what happened.

The first approach is the 'composing' approach. It's the equivalent of a composer working at a desk or piano, scoring a piece of music before handing it on to a band or an orchestra to play.

The second approach is the 'improvising' approach. It's like a folk or jazz musician picking up their instrument and creating a piece out of the scales, chords or riffs that emerge.

In fact, you probably did a bit of both: switching from composing to improvising and back again.

Why design thinking isn't analytical thinking

Constructed problems require a different kind of thinking to presented problems. Rather than finding a fault and removing or repairing it, we identify a goal and find a way to create or achieve it. We move from analytical thinking to design thinking.

Analytical thinking	Design thinking
Starts with a problem	Starts with a solution
Seeks to understand the problem more fully	Seeks to create a more effective solution
Gap between what is and what *should* be	Gap between what is and what *could* be
Breaks the situation into constituent parts	Puts together elements to find the best combination
Examines the present in the context of past events	Tries to create the future using the resources of the present
Asks: 'Is it true?'	Asks: 'Will it work?'

Plans: well-structured constructed problems

Plans are well-structured constructed problems. We can analyse the structure of a constructed problem in just the same way that we analyse a presented problem: by looking at initial conditions, goal conditions, operators and constraints:

- Where are we?
- Where do we want to be?
- How could we get there?
- What limits our options?

If we can answer those questions precisely, we have a plan.

Plans: key features

- Problem statement: 'How to ...'
- There is a gap between what *is* and what *could be* (see Figure 8.1).
- Problem well defined: initial conditions, goal conditions, operators and constraints clear.
- Solution: create something new.
- Leading heuristics: 'how to'; opportunity-led design.

Figure 8.1 The gap

The previous design task is a good example of a plan:

- **Clear initial conditions**: a blank piece of paper and the contents of your wallet or purse.

- **A clear goal**: although there was no correct answer, the *form* of the goal was precise. And the goal was a complete task, not a part of a larger problem.

- **Clear operators**: the rules were simple, and you were in control. Nobody was interfering with your work; you were completely in charge. You were able to start again if you were dissatisfied with your first solution.

- **Clear constraints**: you could use only the resources available. And the solution was going to be evaluated only in one way: aesthetically (not for usefulness or accuracy).

How do we create clear goals for constructed problems? After all, constructed problems can never have single correct solutions. Solutions in design thinking are never correct – they can only ever be acceptable or appropriate. The more clearly we can define criteria of acceptability or appropriateness, the clearer our goal will be.

We use plans to create new things: a cake, a cure for cancer, the iPod, the *Mona Lisa*. The clarity of the goal depends on criteria of acceptability or appropriateness. How good is the cake? Is the patient cured? Do our customers like the new product? Do we have a work of art? The criteria may include definitions that are more or less controversial. Does a cake have to be baked? Does the *Mona Lisa* count as a work of art?

Plans: what styles to use?

 Making plans means using design thinking, so, not surprisingly, the Designer style of problem-solving predominates. We'll also do well to start by using Explorer.

The five stages of design thinking

Design thinking is too important to be left to the Designers. Any constructed problem, in whatever field, is best solved using the basic protocols of design thinking:

1. *Express the problem as a 'how to' statement.*

   As usual, the way we express the problem is critically important. And we need to express it in a form that's conducive to design thinking. We need to define the problem not as something wrong, but as a goal to be achieved.

   And the simple way to do that is to frame the problem as a 'how to' statement. 'Our current invoicing system is lousy' is not a statement conducive to design thinking. 'How to process invoices more efficiently and effectively' puts us in the right starting place.

2. *Generate lots of ideas.*

   We all tend to solve the same problems in the same ways. Those mental models can't help but assert themselves, especially if they were successful in the past. Design thinking demands new ideas. No matter how obviously correct or successful the old solution may seem, we need to generate new solutions if we want to follow design thinking. And the more the better. Generating more than one possible solution can only be beneficial. (Remember the curse of the right answer!)

3. *Refine ideas and build feasibility.*

   Steps 1 and 2 are going to generate lots of ideas. At step 3, we need to take a handful of the most promising potential solutions and work them out in more detail. At this stage, our task is to build feasibility: to develop a solution so that it becomes more practicable. We might combine elements from different solutions, or transfer elements from one to another. A good idea is to pilot a solution and see how it works.

4. *Repeat steps 2 and 3.*

   Design thinking is often iterative. Piloting a solution may show that elements need to be redesigned or thought through afresh. 'Back to the drawing board', indeed. A pilot solution may also reveal important aspects of the original problem that were previously hidden.

5. *Pick the winning solution and implement it.*

   Once we know which solution to carry out, we need to set up the plan to implement it. And guess what? Implementation may throw up new problems requiring more design thinking. So, on it goes.

'How to': goal orientation made simple

Goal orientation is the textbook name for working out what we want to create. The simplest mechanism for putting ourselves in goal orientation mode is to create a 'how to' statement.

You can do this in two ways:

1. You can create it from scratch:
   - how to cook the perfect Quiche Lorraine;
   - how to create an entertaining corporate conference;
   - how to develop a new product.

2. You can take a presented problem and transform it into a 'how to' statement (as we did at the end of the last chapter). Presented problems, as we know, are expressed as statements of what is wrong. Take any such statement and turn it into a 'how to' and the consequences are interesting. For example, *'my client won't accept my proposal'* might become *'how to persuade my client to accept my proposal'*.

Something magical happens when you make the transformation. From focusing on what's wrong, you immediately place the focus of your attention on what *you* can do. You're now involved in the problem and, more importantly, you're committed to doing something.

You probably noticed something else, as soon as you read those two statements. The moment you generate one 'how to' statement, others begin to occur to you. Why 'persuade'? Why not 'make' or 'convince'? And then other 'how to' statements begin to follow, thick and fast:

- *How to win my client's confidence.*
- *How to show the client the benefits of my proposal.*
- *How to compare my proposal to other proposals on my client's desk.*
- *How to arouse my client's enthusiasm.*
- *How to make my client feel they're missing something without my proposal.*
- *How to break down my client's resistance.*

And so on. 'How to' generates multiple possibilities: new ways of thinking about the problem. Some of them will be sub-problems: things you would need to do to achieve the larger goal. Others will be different ways of looking at the problem, including metaphorical or crazy statements that might stimulate more imaginative approaches to the task. Other potential 'how to' statements might be:

- functional aspects (design, production, administration, finance ...);
- different points of view (management, technical, customer, political);
- departments affected (functional, divisional, regional);
- reasons for or causes of the problem; or
- chronological stages or process steps in the problem.

'How to' is a wonderful tool for unsticking your thinking about a problem.

Of course, generating so many ideas can be alarming. How to make sense of this mess? It's important that, at some point, you insist on a single, definitive 'how to' statement that sums up the problem as you see it. After all, without a defining 'how to', you'll be unable to focus your activities into a coherent plan. But the 'how to' that you choose after this period of expansive exploration is likely to be far more interesting and powerful than the 'how to' you began with. All the new 'how to' statements have allowed you to explore different aspects of the problem, including your feelings about it and what you really want to achieve.

What to do

Unsticking your thinking with sticky notes

One way to develop your 'how to' thinking is to use pads of sticky notes. As you generate new 'how to' statements, put each one on a new sticky note. As the number of 'how to' statements increases, you can begin to move the sticky notes around, helping you to see how they relate to each other.

For example, you might decide to cluster the 'how to's into categories. Typical categories might be:

- people
- systems
- processes
- equipment.

Alternatively, you might like to map 'how to' statements into networks of relationships, or process diagrams. You could sort them into trees, made up of main ideas and sub-ideas. Often, the principle of organizing the 'how to's suggests itself as you are working on the problem.

Using sticky notes gives you the freedom to organize and reorganize your ideas as you go. And it often helps you find yet more 'how to' statements!

Shifting perspective: developing 'how to' in four directions

You can develop your 'how to' powers by changing your perspective. And you can shift perspective in four directions (see Figure 8.2).

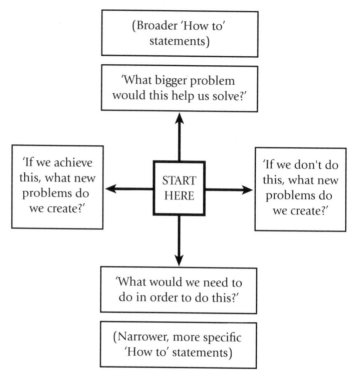

Figure 8.2 The four directions

Shift upwards: what larger problem do we solve?

In this shift, assume that the problem is in fact a solution. You can then ask two questions:

1. What higher-level problem would it solve?
2. What benefits would this solution bring?

These are effectively variants of the same question, but it helps to consider them separately.

For example, suppose the original 'how to' statement was:

> How to check whether the chain carrying the conveyor belt through the spray chamber is at the correct tension, without stopping the conveyor belt

Assume that the problem is a solution. If you could check the chain in this way, what higher-level problem would you solve?

> How to avoid periodically halting the production process to inspect the conveyor chain

And if you could do *that*?

> How to prevent loss of productivity through regular inspections

And?

> How to keep the conveyor belt running continuously

You can ask a similar question by thinking about the benefits of solving the problem. The benefits in this case might include:

- prevention of conveyor slippages due to slack chains;
- prevention of product sprayed wrongly;
- reduced repair costs to the conveyor;

leading to these new 'how to' statements:

- how to keep the conveyor running at a constant speed through the spraying unit;
- how to ensure that all products are sprayed consistently;
- how to reduce repair costs to the conveyor.

In all cases, the new 'how to' statements are broader, more strategic problems. By shifting your perspective on the problem, you've liberated yourself from 'tunnel vision': you're no longer focusing on a specific problem but seeing it potentially as a symptom of a larger problem. By addressing the larger problem, you may be able to solve the original problem and others at the same time.

Shift downwards: how do we achieve this?

This shift, unsurprisingly, takes you in the opposite direction. Instead of assuming that the problem is a solution, ask what you'd need to do in order to achieve the solution.

Suppose the original 'how to' is:

How to increase audience
numbers at our performances

Ask: 'What would we need to do in order to increase audience numbers?' Potential answers might include:

| How to publicize our performances more effectively | How to find new audiences | How to make our performances more attractive |

Each of these new ideas can be broken down further: publicity would include posters, press, media, e-marketing, viral marketing, and so on; finding new audiences might involve contacting schools and colleges, community groups or different age groups; making performances more attractive might include reviewing production policy, front-of-house arrangements, and so on.

In all cases, the original problem is being broken down into more specific, tactical 'how to' statements. Each one is potentially part of a strategic plan to tackle the original problem.

Shifting downwards is potentially the most obvious way to create a plan of action. But there are other perspective shifts and they, too, can be useful.

Shift sideways: if we don't do this, what problems do we face?

In this shift, consider the consequences of *not* doing what you're thinking about. What problems would you face – new or already existing?

For example, suppose your original problem were:

| How to increase the speed of migration of our client database to the new operating platform |

What if you couldn't migrate your client information more quickly to the new operating platform? What problems, new or existing, would you face? Among the possible problems, you might include:

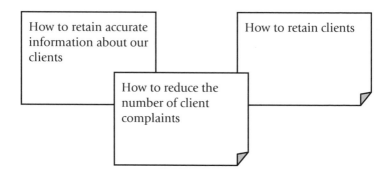

How to retain accurate information about our clients

How to retain clients

How to reduce the number of client complaints

These new ideas are potentially extremely useful in developing contingency or protective measures to make your plan more robust.

Shift sideways: if we achieve this, what new problems do we create?

All plans will have consequences. Some of them will be undesirable. (Remember wicked problems in the last chapter?) By shifting perspective in this direction, you may be able to foresee some of those problems and plan to manage or avoid them.

For example, suppose your original 'how to' is:

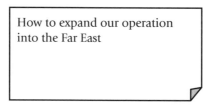

How to expand our operation into the Far East

However attractive it might be to access the huge and booming markets of Asia, solving this problem might generate all sorts of new problems, such as:

How to ensure reliable delivery of products across large distances

How to expand our production capacity

How to align our products and marketing to cultural values in our new markets

Once again, the new ideas you generate by shifting perspective help you to make your plans more robust.

Focusing your attention systematically in this way will help you to deepen your understanding of the problem and develop more thorough plans.

The pleasures and perils of planning

Planning, they say, is the process of preparing, making and managing change. Having decided what to do (which 'how to' you are going to pursue), the next step is to plan a route from where you are to where you want to be – from initial conditions to goal conditions. The plan you create is the set of operators that will help you achieve your chosen solution.

And yet, we all know that plans sometimes fall apart disastrously. Why? And what can we learn from all the plans that go wrong?

The traditional advice: plan backwards

When thinking about a plan of action it's most natural, in the words of Lewis Carroll, to 'begin at the beginning and go on 'till you come to the end, then stop'. And, if you've read project management textbooks, you'll know that you need to establish 'milestones' – places you need to reach by a certain point if you're to stay on track.

The advantage of planning backwards is that you start with the goal in mind. With the success of your goal clearly in focus, you can then map out the actions needed to get there, and the milestones you will need to cross on your way.

Waterfall planning

Wise project-planning consultants tell us that project planning is itself always subject to change. Trevor Young – one of the wisest – writes in one of his books:

"Certainly, the planning process is dynamic and continuous. You will still be planning some of the finer points of detail of the last part of the project even during the rundown stage.**"**

Nonetheless, the traditional wisdom of project planning still often ignores the need for messy adaptability. Instead, it develops backward planning into something often called the 'waterfall model': a neat, linear sequence of stages, each of which should be completed before we embark on the next (see Figure 8.3).

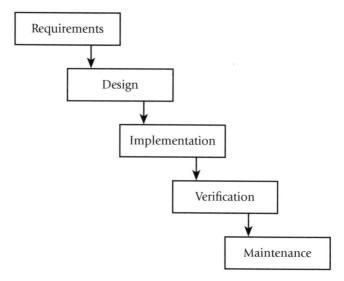

Figure 8.3 The waterfall model

Developed for use in the highly structured worlds of manufacturing and construction, the waterfall model has become a fairly standard model for projects in other fields, such as information technology, administration, education and healthcare. Every time you see a Gannt chart on a manager's wall, you can be certain that the waterfall model is at work.

But is it effective?

Business projects are notoriously unsuccessful. Survey after survey reports that high proportions of projects fail to fulfil their brief, fail to deliver the promised return on investment and fail to add value to the business. And the reasons that they fail often have to do with the inability of the planning process to accommodate the wickedness of the problem.

It's a question of context. The waterfall model may work in a closed system such as an assembly plant, where the problem parameters are closely defined. But if the context of the problem is more open, a neat linear progression from one stage to the next is unlikely to happen.

Wicked problems demand wicked planning.

When business intelligence projects lack intelligence

Most of the statistics about project management these days relate to information technology – sometimes called 'business intelligence', or BI.

A 2011 report by Gartner, an IT analyst, suggests that 'between 70% to 80% of corporate business intelligence projects fail'. And the key reason, it seems, is that IT departments look at BI as an engineering problem rather than a business problem.

In other words, they are thinking 'waterfall' and ignoring the wickedness of the problem.

The first step, according to Patrick Meehan, president and research director in Gartner's CIO Research group, is to find out what the business really needs: 'If you don't ask the right questions, BI is not a crystal ball that pops out the answer. People in IT need to stop approaching BI as a vendor or engineering solution, or as a tool. They need to understand what business they are in. They are in the information and communication business.'

Opportunity-led thinking

So, while the waterfall model can be put to good use within nice neat closed systems, it shouldn't be used without careful thought about its effectiveness in your particular situation. For example, it doesn't reflect the way we actually go about designing things.

Think back to making your design at the start of this chapter. Did you follow the waterfall model? How carefully did you consider the requirements of the task before beginning to design? How much did you design in your head before putting the pieces together?

My guess is that your thinking worked rather differently. You were negotiating in your mind between what you wanted to achieve, and what you could do. Whenever we're creating something new, we have one eye on what we want to create, and another on what we have and what we can do (see Figure 8.4). The gap between the two creates a tension that we try to resolve by taking action.

Every need has a cost. Some needs will be more expensive to achieve than others; achieving more needs will probably cost more than achieving fewer needs. Designing a car that will protect its passengers in a 40mph head-on collision may cost more than designing a car that will protect its driver in a 30mph lateral collision. Successful design thinking is always a matter of balancing priorities: creating solutions that are new, feasible *and* cost-effective. It's a tough combination to crack, but that's what we're trying to do.

The way to plan forwards is to look for opportunities to resolve the tension.

That's not an analytical process. It's not entirely rational. We're looking for the combinations of elements that will balance all the priorities most effectively. And looking for combinations is as much intuitive as it is rational.

We know that if we try too hard to understand all the needs we're trying to fulfil, we're likely to get stuck. The technical term is 'analysis paralysis': we can't take action until we have more information, but we can't get more information until we take action.

To avoid analysis paralysis, try to find opportunities to create a solution. It's called 'opportunity-led' thinking. Create possible solutions and see how they might work. Then adjust your search on the basis of what you find. All the time you're looking for the places where you can make headway, backing up when an opportunity leads to a dead end, pushing forwards when it promises help.

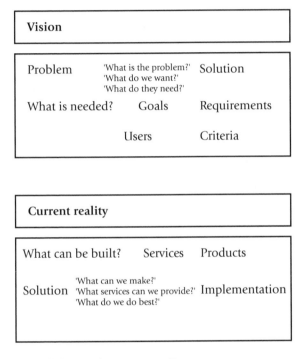

Figure 8.4 Vision and current reality

And if this reminds you of the intuitive problem-solving cycle we explored in Chapter 1 – well, that's exactly what it is.

The resulting activity can look pretty chaotic (see Figure 8.5), but in fact it's very well organized. You're switching your focus of attention back and forth between your vision and current reality – between what you want and what you've got. You're trying to make the most headway possible, regardless of where the headway happens, by making opportunity-led switches the focus of your attention.

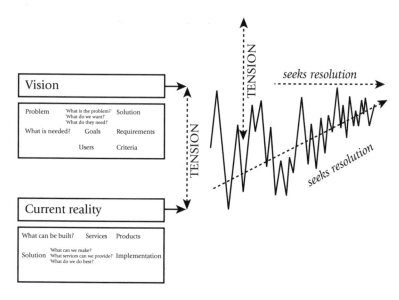

Figure 8.5 Switching between vision and current reality

In design thinking, we need to be able to *recognize* a good solution when we stumble upon it.

Welcoming chaos into your project plans

Almost any project plan needs to include space for opportunity-led design thinking.

The waterfall model will work if – and only if – we're solving a problem within a closed system. (Look back at Chapter 7, in particular the section on 'modelling the problem system'.) If we can define the problem precisely, if we know precisely what the solution must look like and if we have the tools and experience to solve it – then a strictly linear plan, drawn up as a neat Gannt chart, will work.

Many problems, as we've seen, are wicked – the context of the problem is not closed but open and subject to change. The key factor in what makes a problem wicked is usually people. And people, on the whole, are pretty unpredictable.

So if you're designing a solution that involves users, customers or colleagues, then you'll need to operate within a framework that can accommodate a degree of chaos.

Easier said than done, of course. Imagine you're a project leader: you're responsible for keeping the project to time and within budget. If the project fails to meet all the requirements in the brief, you'll be accountable. You know that the process will – *must* – include opportunity-led thinking, but you must still make plans, create schedules and commit to milestones. Officially, you're in charge of keeping the project on the waterfall line. It can be hard to loosen your control of a project and face the prospect of seemingly chaotic activity.

The key is to recognize when such thinking is necessary and to manage it dynamically. The control you need isn't so much the control of a driver handling a machine, as the control of a surfer riding a wave. It's the dynamic control that balances forces and looks always for the way forward.

From waterfalls to agility: how design thinking is evolving in software design

Software designers are acutely aware of the need to plan more effectively when creating solutions to wicked problems.

Creating a new piece of software to fit into an already existing system is nearly always a wicked problem. Users may not know exactly what they need before looking at a new piece of software. Software designers, on the other hand, can misunderstand users' needs. The result can be software that fails to deliver on its potential or simply replicates what the old software did.

Agile Software Development was founded by a group of software developers in 2001 to address these problems. The Agile Manifesto, in its entirety, reads:

▶

'We are uncovering better ways of developing software by doing it and helping others do it. Through this work we have come to value:

- **individuals and interactions** over processes and tools
- **working software** over comprehensive documentation
- **customer collaboration** over contract negotiation
- **responding to change** over following a plan.'

This is as concise a description of good design thinking as you could get.

Putting design thinking to work every day

Design thinking is an increasingly vital skill. Unfortunately, it's not a skill we're much taught at school.

Edward de Bono, the inventor of – among other things – lateral thinking, has much to say on this subject. In an article for the *Guardian* in 1997, he claimed that 'we prefer critical to constructive thinking, argument to design'. In part, he blames the influence of the 'Gang of Three': Socrates ('who was mostly concerned with proving things wrong'), Plato ('an arrogant Athenian authoritarian') and Aristotle ('with his word-based inclusion/exclusion logic'). According to de Bono, these three proclaimed that 'knowledge is all' and prioritized truth over what he calls 'operacy': 'We are almost totally obsessed with "what is". We underestimate the extremely valuable contribution that "what may be" has made to progress.' As a result, our education system is systematically failing our young people. 'The skills of action are every bit as important as the skills of knowing. We neglect them completely and turn out students who have little to contribute to society.'

De Bono may express himself in extreme terms, but he recognizes that design thinking is a vital element of problem-solving. 'Most of the world's major problems', he writes, 'will not be solved by yet more analysis and yet more information. We need to design ways forward.'

What to do

Improve your operacy skills

Here are 10 ideas that you could apply every day:

1 **Synthesize**. Balance any analytical work you do with synthetic thinking. Look for connections, similarities and analogies. Seek methods of using information in new ways, and in new contexts.

2 **Learn how to learn (fast)**. Information overload is here to stay. Work out how you best create what you know. Schedule your knowledge work carefully so that you build in 'absorption time': naps, exercise, variation in types of work.

3 **Always have a long-term plan**. Planning and design go hand in hand. Making a plan is always worth it, even if you change it every day. In fact, the best reason for making a plan is so that you *can* revise it. And learn more about the problem as you do so.

4 **Plan flexibly**. Use backward planning: be clear about your goal when you are solving a problem. Recognize when your thinking is opportunity-led and allow time to explore.

5 **Map connections**. Draw all your plans out on a large piece of paper; highlight the things that depend on other things. Find the things that don't depend on anything but which have the most dependencies – and concentrate on them.

6 **Collaborate**. One of the most important skills. Very few plans can be achieved by one person. You'll need help, and you'll need it often. Learn the skills of collaboration. Nurture your network of useful working relationships; you never know when you might need them.

7 **Make mistakes, and make them fast**. You're going to mess up; do it quickly and move on. Opportunity-led thinking is all about learning from experience; without having a go, you won't learn. Try to make use of mistakes. To quote the great jazz guitarist, Joe Pass: 'If you hit a wrong note, make it right by what you play afterwards.'

▶

8 **Keep everything**. Document what works. Write up protocols of best practice; keep early drafts; throw nothing away. If you don't record it, it may never have an impact on the world. Much of creativity is learning how to see things properly. Most profound scientific discoveries are surprises. But if you don't document and digest every observation and learn to trust your eyes, then you will not know when you have seen a surprise.

9 **Recycle.** There's only so much time and energy available for invention. If you can use what you created earlier, go ahead.

10 **Seek simplicity**. If it looks hard to do, it probably is. Spend time looking for a dozen ways to make it simpler. You'll save time later; it'll work better; the world will be a better place for it. Albert Einstein was once asked why he used the same soap for washing and for shaving. His reply: 'Two soaps? That's too complicated.'

In brief

Plans: key features

- Problem statement: 'How to ...'
- There is a gap between what *is* and what *could be*.
- Problem well defined: initial conditions, goal conditions, operators and constraints clear.
- Solution: create something new.
- Leading heuristics: 'how to'; opportunity-led design.

Design thinking typically follows an iterative process:

1 **Express the problem as a 'how to' statement.**

2 Generate lots of ideas.

3 Refine ideas and build feasibility.

4 **Repeat steps 2 and 3.**

5 Pick the winning solution and implement it.

We can develop the 'how to' operation by shifting our perspective in four directions:

1 **Shift upwards: if we achieve this, what larger problem do we solve?**

2 **Shift downwards: how do we achieve this?**

3 **Shift sideways: if we don't achieve this, what problems do we face?**

4 **Shift sideways: if we achieve this, what new problems do we create?**

Most projects demand design thinking. Many project plans follow the waterfall model. This model works only when planning within closed systems. When the problem's context is open, opportunity-led thinking is necessary.

Opportunity-led thinking seeks to resolve the gap between vision and reality: between what we want to create and our current resources, by looking for opportunities to act.

In design thinking we need to be able to recognize a good solution when we stumble upon it.

Many problems can be solved only with the skills of operacy.

Chapter

9

Dreaming the future: creative problem-solving

Read this story all the way through, at least once, and then answer the questions.

An oil well in the Arabian desert exploded. The oil company was faced with an inferno consuming vast quantities of oil every day. All efforts to extinguish the fire failed. Eventually, the company called in Flash Quencher, the famed fire-fighter.

Flash could see that the way to quench the fire was to dump a huge quantity of fire-retardant foam at the base of the well. Although there was sufficient foam on site to do the job, the company didn't have a hose large enough to deliver the foam quickly enough. The small hoses on site were simply inadequate.

Flash knew what to do. He stationed men in a circle around the well, each with a hose. All the hoses were opened up at once, and foam was directed at the fire from all sides. The blaze was put out and Flash earned $3 million.

Does this story describe a presented problem or a constructed problem?

Is the problem well structured or ill structured?

List the:

- initial conditions;
- goal conditions;
- operators; and
- constraints.

A dream is an ill-structured constructed problem. It's expressed exactly like a plan: as a 'how to' statement. Unlike a plan, however, a dream solution is not well defined. Indeed, we may not be able to define the problem itself clearly. We may not know exactly where we are, or where we want to go. We may not have any idea how to create our dream: the operators are unclear. We may feel all sorts of constraints: budget, resources, time, regulations. And other constraints may be at work, of which we are unaware: unchallenged assumptions about how things work, how to get results, 'how we do things around here'.

Dreams: key features

- Problem statement: 'How to ...'
- There is a gap between what *is* and what *could be*.
- Problem ill structured: initial conditions, goal conditions, operators and/or constraints unclear.
- Solution: create something new.
- Leading heuristics: 'how to'; associative thinking; metaphor; reversal.

Typical examples of dream problems might be:

- *How to make our products more attractive to our customers.*
- *How to invent a new, healthy fast-food recipe.*
- *How to get on better with a problematic colleague.*
- *How to be more successful.*

To tackle a dream 'how to', we have to find new ways of thinking about it. The aim is not to see the 'how to' more clearly, but to see it *differently*. In other words, we need to be able to *reframe*. (We investigated reframing in Chapter 1.)

Dreams: what styles to use?

Dreams demand the kind of thinking that generates new ideas. Call it 'creative thinking'.

Making dreams come true demands a combination of Explorer and Designer skills.

What to do

Six steps towards being more creative

Based on a number of studies, creativity seems to be a combination of six competencies. Develop your skills in these areas and see yourself become more creative.

Look for problems. Find the unanswered questions, the most awkward problems, the toughest conundrum and the next challenge. Develop your love of research and your hunger for information.

Become mentally mobile. Find different ways of looking at situations. Become adept at turning ideas inside out or back to front. Ask 'What if?'. Challenge assumptions. Fall in love with metaphors. Look for the unusual way to describe a problem.

Take risks. Live a little more dangerously. Look for excitement and stimulation. Seek out unknown territory. Lower your boredom threshold. Improvise. Learn to love failure. Find the edge of your competence and try to live there more often.

Develop a personal aesthetic. Look for patterns, associations and resemblances. Take complexity and try to simplify it. Become comfortable with ambiguity, asymmetry and uncertainty.

▶

> **Be objective about your own work.** Ask others to critique your work and integrate their thoughts into your future efforts. Become hungry for feedback.
>
> **Do what motivates you for its own sake.** Choose the tasks that arouse your passion. Forget rewards, salary or perks. Become impatient of supervision.

We associate creativity with inspiration and genius: factors that are difficult to replicate or to learn. But creative thinking is as organized as any other kind of thinking. We can learn to do it, and we can use it to generate real and useful solutions. In this chapter, we'll discover how.

Mindsets: the good news and the bad news

As we've seen throughout this book, our brains use mental models to explore the world. We assimilate new information to the mental models that have worked in the past, adjusting them occasionally and applying them in new situations to get results. The mental models that work well for us become stronger; the mental models that are less successful become weaker or disappear.

The strongest mental models become mindsets.

Mindsets are an essential part of thinking. They create the assumptions without which thinking wouldn't be possible. They create the routines, protocols and procedures by which we do most of what we do. Without mindsets, we wouldn't be able to get through a day; each operational task would become a new problem, and we would be overwhelmed with potential solutions.

The power of mindsets: part one

Take a moment to count the number of pieces of clothing you put on this morning. Include jewellery, watches and other accessories. (Pairs count as one.) How many possible ways are there of putting on your clothes? (The answer is on page 216.) How many did you consider before starting to get dressed this morning?

The danger with mindsets is that they limit our ability to reframe. Mindsets tell us what to look for, what to see, how to interpret it and what to do. If information fails to fit the mindset, we're more likely to question or reject the information than to question the mindset. We may not even *see* the information.

You walk into a crowded bar, search desperately for an empty seat, find one and sit down. Two minutes later your friends make their way to your table and ask why on earth you ignored them. They were waving frantically, but you ignored them completely. The mindset of looking for a free seat blinded you – literally – to their attention-seeking gestures.

The most well-known study demonstrating the power of mindsets to blind us to information was conducted in the late 1990s by Daniel Simons of the University of Illinois and Christopher Chabris of Harvard University. They asked subjects to watch a short video in which two groups of people pass a basketball around. The subjects were told to count the number of bounce passes and aerial passes between team members. After watching the video, the subjects were asked if they'd noticed anything unusual. About half the subjects had failed to spot a woman wearing a full gorilla suit crossing the field of view. (Another version involves a woman carrying an umbrella.) The mindset established by the task – carefully counting ball passes – had completely blinded these people to the unusual event in front of their eyes.

Because mindsets so powerfully frame the way we see reality, they can severely constrain our ability to solve problems where reframing is needed.

Danger! Mindsets at work!

Mindsets are at work continuously. By focusing on the mental models that govern how we operate, we risk missing the opportunities to discover new solutions. Here are some obvious examples:

- **Product development:** focus on engineering the product rather than looking for different ways of satisfying the customer.
- **Introducing new IT systems:** designing on the basis of existing IT solutions rather than defining user requirements and designing to satisfy them.
- **Contractual negotiations:** discussing preconceived 'issues' rather than addressing the assumptions on both sides about what the issues might be and how they have arisen.
- **Responding to customer complaints:** regarding the complaint as 'something to be dealt with' rather than an opportunity to improve a product or service.
- **Quality management:** looking for defects rather than building in quality.
- **Strategy:** 're-engineering' an organizational structure rather than asking 'What business are we in?'.

Operational thinking and creative thinking

We spend most of our active time in a cycle of doing, evaluating, reflecting, planning and re-doing (see Figure 9.1).

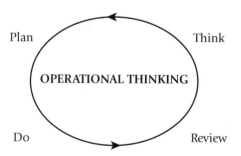

Figure 9.1 The operational cycle

As we travel the operational cycle, we use protocols, procedures and routines: mindsets that regulate our behaviour. They help us to work efficiently; they help us to improve our processes and to use resources well.

But when we are looking for new ideas, these routines become limiting frames on our thinking. We need to reframe in order to explore new possibilities. We need to leave the operational cycle and cross into the creative cycle (see figure below).

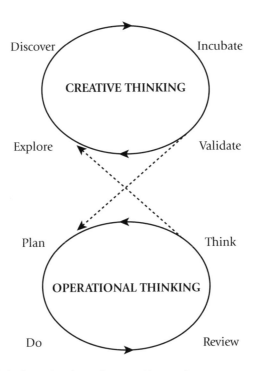

Figure 9.2 Crossing into the creative cycle

These two cycles have radically different aims. The aim of the operational cycle is to improve what we do. The aim of the creative cycle is to *find something different to do*. The principal thinking styles in the operational cycle are to:

- plan;
- act (to carry out the plan);
- review what we've done;
- think about what the review has told us; and
- adjust the plan so that future action is improved.

The principal thinking styles in the creative cycle are to:

- explore;
- discover;
- incubate (think about what we've discovered); and
- validate (develop what we've discovered into something useful).

Joseph Campbell, the great mythographer, once defined creativity as 'going out to find the thing society hasn't found yet'. The creative cycle is the process of discovering something new and useful that we can bring back into the operational cycle.

Most of us think and work in the creative thinking cycle only occasionally. It's unlikely that any of us would think 'outside the box' as a matter of course (unless our operational work demanded it of us – as designers, performers or scientists, perhaps). Indeed, there are usually only two circumstances in which we'll cross from the operational cycle into the creative cycle:

1. because we have to; or
2. because we choose to.

It may take a crisis to force us to move into creative thinking. If a relationship is in danger of collapsing, we might have to reframe our assumptions about it. If a company is facing bankruptcy, we may have to come up with creative solutions for keeping the enterprise afloat or to reinvent it. Unfortunately, crises tend to be emotionally fraught and thus not always the best time to engage in creative thinking.

But we can always *choose* to leave the operational cycle behind for a while and do some creative thinking. We can engage in thought experiments; we can run brainstorming sessions; we can run a research project or a pilot.

To cross successfully into the creative cycle, we need to be relaxed and safe. We need to be in a place where we can feel free to think the unthinkable, and where we can manage risk. Airline pilots wouldn't try out new ways of controlling a plane while actually flying a jet; they'd use a flight simulator. Similarly, if we want to generate new ideas, we need a 'flight simulator' – a secure environment where we can break the rules safely.

The two cycles – operational and creative – are separate. We can't do creative thinking in the operational cycle, and operational thinking is unhelpful in the creative cycle. One of the greatest dangers in thinking about dreams is that we may find ourselves trying to think in both cycles at the same time. The classic symptom of trying to think in both cycles simultaneously is the emergence of 'idea killers' – operational responses to new ideas generated by creative thinking.

What to do

20 idea killers

Listen out for these responses when you're trying to generate new ideas. They are key signs that you are slipping back into the operational cycle.

Not practical.

It'll never work.

Let's wait a bit.

Too complicated.

What's the point?

That reminds me …

It'll cost too much.

It'll never catch on.

What about the intangibles?

You haven't thought it through.

▶

> We tried it before and it didn't work.
>
> That's a bit too radical for this company.
>
> You'll never get people to change their ways.
>
> I like the idea, but I'm not sure that my boss ...
>
> That isn't quite the way we do things around here.
>
> The idea isn't relevant to our current strategic planning.
>
> Good idea. We shall appoint a working party to look into it.
>
> Of course, that's just the sort of idea we might expect from you.
>
> Hm. Now, suppose we changed this little bit, and that little bit, and ...
>
> We don't have the resources/staff/money/time/expertise/room/systems ...

Intuition revisited: training to reframe

Most reframing happens unconsciously. Remember the Rubin vase in Chapter 1 (see page 18)? Most of us can reframe that image with no effort, and without consciously thinking about it.

Because reframing is usually unconscious, we might feel that we can do little to develop it as a conscious skill. Someone might jolt us into reframing a problem – by asking us 'to look at it another way' or shouting at us to 'look at it from my point of view – for a change!'.

Roger van Oech, creativity consultant and author, calls these moments 'whacks on the side of the head'. We can look for more opportunities to give ourselves whacks on the side of the head; and, in fact, there's a lot more we can do to help our intuitive mind to reframe more efficiently.

The first skill we can develop is the ability to prepare ourselves for those moments when reframing might occur.

Archimedes in the bath

The most famous story of intuitive problem-solving is the tale of Archimedes in the bath.

Archimedes of Syracuse (c 287BC – c 212BC) was one of the leading scientists of antiquity. According to Vitruvius (a Roman writing 200 years later), King Hiero II of Syracuse had donated pure gold to make a votive crown for a temple in the city. The king suspected that a rogue goldsmith had adulterated the gold with silver, and asked Archimedes to find out if the crown was indeed pure gold.

Thinking about the problem, Archimedes transformed it. Impure gold has a lower density than pure gold. Density is weight per unit volume. Archimedes knew the density of pure gold, and he could easily weigh the crown. All he needed to know was its volume.

But calculating the volume of an intricately irregular solid like a crown was no easy task. There was no way he could melt the crown down into a regular shape.

Archimedes was stuck.

So, like any good thinker, he took a break and visited the local baths. As he sank into the warm, relaxing water, he noticed that his own irregularly shaped body displaced its own volume of water – and he could do the same with the crown to measure its volume. Divide the crown's weight by its volume, and Archimedes would find the metal's density. Problem solved.

So excited was Archimedes by this discovery that he leapt from his bath and ran through the streets naked, crying 'Eureka!' (which is Greek for 'I've found it!').

And apparently the goldsmith had indeed added silver to the gold. Good news for Archimedes; bad news for the goldsmith.

The four stages of reframing

Over 2000 years after Archimedes, a socialist and educationalist called Graham Wallas formalized reframing into a four-part model:

1. Preparation (conscious work on a problem).
2. Incubation (internalization of the problem context and goals into the subconscious, where the problem is processed).
3. Illumination (when reframing occurs: the 'eureka' moment).
4. Verification and elaboration (checking that the insight is valid and then developing it into a workable solution).

Wallas's model suggests that reframing is more likely to happen when our conscious, rational minds are relaxed.

How good are you at reframing?

Here's a problem that needs a creative solution. Study the problem carefully and then see if any possible solution occurs to you.

You're a doctor with a patient who has a malignant stomach tumour. Unless you can destroy the tumour, the patient will die. You have at your disposal a kind of ray that you can use to destroy the tumour, if the rays hit the tumour at a sufficiently high intensity. Unfortunately, at the required intensity the rays will also destroy any healthy tissue they pass through. At lower intensities the rays are harmless to healthy tissue but will not affect the tumour. What type of procedure could you use to destroy the tumour with the rays, without destroying the healthy tissue?

If you have immediately solved the problem, well done! If not, let me give you some instructions.

First, express the problem as a 'how to' statement. How well structured is the problem in the form in which you've expressed it? Initial conditions and goal conditions are both clear: the presence and absence of the tumour, respectively. The lack of structure seems to arise with operators: how many ways can you think of to use the rays?

If you have solved the problem by this point, well done. If not, let me give you a hint.

Is there anything that you've read so far in this chapter that might help you solve this problem?

And if that hasn't nudged your thinking, let me try a hefty whack on the side of your head.

Could you use the oil well problem at the start of this chapter to help you?

At some point in the last few lines, I hope you've had a 'eureka' moment. You suddenly realized that the Flash Quencher story could supply the solution to the tumour problem: where Flash used hoses in a circular arrangement to focus low amounts of foam on one point, you could administer low-density rays from different directions to destroy the tumour without damaging the surrounding tissue.

You've reframed: the same principle, in different contexts, has helped you to solve the problem.

Put another way, the oil well story has become a metaphor for the tumour problem. (More about metaphors shortly.)

Now: did you reframe without a hint from me? If you did, then I salute your powers of intuition. When Mary Gick and Keith Holyoak conducted a very similar experiment in the late 1970s, they found that fewer than 10% of their volunteers used the story to solve the problem without a hint. Given a hint by the research team, however, 75% successfully reframed.

Life, of course, tends not to give us hints. Without guidance, we might never make the new connections that allow us to reframe a problem. Are we condemned, then, to simply wait for the moments when reframing happens? How can we train ourselves to reframe a bit more systematically?

As the great sci-fi writer Philip K. Dick said: 'Look where you least expect to find it.' It sounds paradoxical: how can we look for the unexpected? Or rather: *when* do we look for the unexpected?

When we explore. When we go on holiday, on an excursion, on an expedition into the unknown. Exploration is the systematic search for the unexpected. If you go where you've already been, you'll find what you've already found. To find something truly new: explore. That's why the first step on the creative cycle is to explore.

And there are techniques available to help us do just that.

Associative thinking

Reframing techniques have gone by various names over the years. The basic term is 'associative thinking'. We link items in our minds by making associations with them: perhaps because they are similar, because they are closely linked, or because they are opposites. It's easy to do, and it can be more useful than you might think, especially in pursuit of dream solutions. Reframing creates new and unexpected associations, which are the 'creative sparks' of new ideas.

Making the links: a mental diversion

We can link items in our minds in three ways (for the moment!):

1. similarity;
2. closeness;
3. opposition.

For example, we might link the word 'apple' to:

- orange (similar);
- tree (closeness); or
- poison (opposition: I'm thinking of Snow White, fooled by the wicked queen's poisoned apple).

Sometimes, one kind of link is easier to find than another. (What's the opposite of an apple?) That doesn't really matter. Associative thinking is not concerned with finding the right answer. (And, in that respect, it's the opposite of rational thinking, with its curse of the right answer.) *Any* answer that makes a new link is acceptable when we're thinking associatively. The only rule is that we should try to look for surprising links (that paradox, again): the more surprising the link, the greater the likelihood of reframing.

Making the link: exercising your powers of associative thinking

Here are some more words, chosen at random. Can you create some associative links?

	Similar	Close	Opposite
Gasp			
Urge			
Font			
Edge			
Tube			
Nightmare			
Sun			
Golf			
Year			
Birth			

Most creativity techniques involve associative thinking in pursuit of reframing. Broadly, they fall into two categories: techniques involving **metaphor** (looking for similarities and closeness); and techniques involving **reversal** (looking for opposites).

Metaphor: what you see is – something else

What have the following all got in common?

An industry watchdog

The University of Life

A hive of activity

The ship of state

Cashflow

A ribbon development

A cast-iron guarantee

The answer, of course, is that they are all metaphors. A metaphor reframes instantly: it allows us to see something in terms of something else. By describing a nation state as a ship, or a financial instrument in terms of heavy engineering, we can look at these things differently.

We've long realized how important metaphor is in solving problems. Stephen Mithen, whom we met in Chapter 2, sees metaphor as key to the cognitive fluidity that opens up the cathedral of the human mind. Spanish philosopher Ortega y Gasset calls metaphor 'probably the most fertile power possessed by men'. Metaphor is certainly one of the core tools of creative thinking.

I remember, on my first trip to Crete, seeing the word on a sign at the airport: μεταθοραι (metaphorai), meaning 'transport'; and then, a few minutes later, on the side of a lorry (meaning 'logistics'). Greece: the land where metaphors roam the streets!

New worlds: finding unusual metaphors to work with

One way to make our thinking more metaphorical is to place a problem in a different world. We might categorize these worlds broadly as 'organic' and 'inorganic'. If the problem is 'organic' – if it involves people, for example, or biological systems – we can invoke a metaphor from the inorganic world (suppose our organization were a galaxy of stars?). If the problem is technical, we could find an organic metaphor (what if an airline catering trolley were an animal?).

Switching radically between worlds can provide more interesting and provocative metaphors.

Organic		Inorganic	
Biology	Theatre	Physics	Oceanography
Tribal customs	Education	Mineralogy	Geology
Sports	Animals	Woodworking	Architecture
Fashion	Politics	Chemistry	Meteorology
Dancing	Racing	Mathematics	Bridges
War	Espionage	Electricity	Aeronautics
History	Comedy	Astronomy	Transport
Mythology	Agriculture	Machines	Acoustics
Botany	Finance	Rocks	Archaeology
Philosophy	Science Fiction	Metalworking	Time and space

Consulting the oracle: metaphors at work

An oracle is a metaphor-making tool. Oracles use randomly generated information to help us think associatively. They invite us to look at an idea in terms of something else. We're unlikely to make new mental connections using our existing mental models and memories; we need randomly generated information to help us make new links, reframe and find new ideas.

We love oracles. We read our horoscopes. We shuffle Tarot cards and throw dice. In ancient times, people visited oracles in places such as Delphi, where priests or priestesses would utter strange pronouncements in answer to their questions.

What to do

A do-it-yourself oracle

The easiest way to make your own oracle is to use randomly generated words. Key the phrase 'random word generator' into your search engine and you'll soon find one. The generator will offer you randomly selected words that you can juxtapose against a problem to stimulate new ideas.

▶

For example, suppose the problem is:

How to encourage my team to be more creative

I generated four words on a random word generator:

- **Salon:** how about establishing a creativity salon or room, where the team can use toys and games to stimulate new ideas?

- **Curry:** how about finding ways of mixing different ingredients into projects or team activities to spark creativity?

- **Captain:** does the team need leadership to help it unlock its creativity?

- **Roof:** maybe we need an overarching strategy that integrates creativity into team objectives and competencies.

The best words for this kind of associative thinking are concrete nouns: words that name things physically present in the world. Concrete nouns stimulate our imagination with images, and the images create powerful sparks. Words like 'finance', 'planning' or 'region' are not likely to be so rich in associations.

The intermediate impossible: reversal as an idea generator

A second set of techniques uses the idea of *reversal* to give our thinking a nudge.

Reversal means turning a problem inside out, upside down or back to front. The idea is that, if we deliberately imagine the direct opposite of what we want to achieve, we may find new ways of looking at it.

For example, if we were considering 'how to improve customer satisfaction with our helpline', we might start to generate new 'how to' statements that are deliberately the *reverse* of what we want to achieve:

- *How to reduce customer satisfaction with our helpline.*
- *How to enrage our customers.*
- *How to scare our customers.*
- *How to chase our customers away with no solution.*
- *How to be as unhelpful as possible.*

And so on.

Such crazy ideas may hold within them the seeds of a new, useful idea. For example:

- **How to reduce customer satisfaction with our helpline**: *how about giving customers more information so that they need to ring the helpline less?*
- **How to enrage our customers**: *how about finding the key sources of dissatisfaction when customers call the helpline, and train helpline staff to identify them; how about improving our anger management techniques?*
- **How to scare our customers**: *how about explaining more clearly to customers the consequences of doing something wrong?*
- **How to chase our customers away with no solution**: *how about giving customers more tools to solve their own problems?*
- **How to be as unhelpful as possible**: *how about focusing more on the diagnostic stage of a customer call, before leaping to suggestions for help?*

People sometimes find reversal techniques harder to use than metaphorical ones. Reversal challenges our deepest assumptions, and that can be uncomfortable. However, with practice, reversal can be great fun. Thinking up the most outrageous negative ideas can become a competitive game (the key to winning, in my experience, is to think up an idea that offends the rules of physics). The aim of the technique is to find what Edward de Bono calls 'intermediate impossibles': ideas that are as *im*possible as we can make them, which can act as intermediate stages on the lateral journey from problem to new idea.

The power of mindsets: part two

How many possible ways are there of putting on your clothes? (We asked this question on page 201).

The answer is simply the multiple of all the numbers up to your chosen number of pieces of clothing.

For example, if you put on eight pieces of clothing this morning, the number of possible ways of getting dressed is:

$8 \times 7 \times 6 \times 5 \times 4 \times 3 \times 2 \times 1 = 40,320$

Of course, some operations are not allowable: we don't usually put on socks over shoes or underwear over trousers or skirts. But even a tenth of the number presents a formidable array of options. The mindset we develop over the years helps us to ignore all the possibilities. Without it, we'd still be wondering how to get dressed at bedtime.

In brief

Dreams: key features

- Problem statement: 'How to ...'
- There is a gap between what *is* and what *could be*.
- Problem ill structured: initial conditions, goal conditions, operators and/or constraints unclear.
- Solution: create something new.
- Leading heuristics: 'how to'; associative thinking; metaphor; reversal.

Dreams demand creative thinking. Creative thinking breaks mindsets (the mental models that create the assumptions without which thinking wouldn't be possible). Mindsets help operational thinking, but they are a powerful constraint on creative thinking.

To think creatively, we need to leave the operational cycle and cross into the creative cycle. The aim of the operational cycle is to improve what we do. The aim of the creative cycle is to *find something different to do*. We only cross into the creative cycle because we have to, or because we choose to.

Creative thinking involves reframing: seeing the same element of reality through a different mental model. The reframing process has been codified into four stages:

1 preparation (conscious work on a problem);
2 incubation;
3 illumination;
4 verification and elaboration.

Reframing uses associative thinking. We can create associations in terms of:

- similarity;
- closeness;
- opposition.

▶

Most creativity techniques use associative thinking. Broadly, they fall into two categories: techniques involving **metaphor** (looking for similarities and closeness); and techniques involving **reversal**.

Chapter

10

Making it happen: deciding wisely

"If an important decision is to be made, they discuss the question when they are drunk, and the following day the master of the house where the discussion was held submits their decision for reconsideration when they are sober. If they still approve it, it is adopted; if not, it is abandoned. Conversely, any decision they make when they are sober is reconsidered afterwards when they are drunk.**"**

This is Herodotus, the 'father of History', writing about the Persians. Being Greek, Herodotus regarded the Persians as fascinating foreigners, with strange habits.

The first half of Herodotus' description is easily recognizable. We all know how we can make stupid, impetuous decisions when drunk or emotionally aroused; and we know that it usually pays to sober up and 'sleep on it' before we finally decide.

What's intriguing, though, is the second half of Herodotus' account. His Persians don't only submit their drunken decisions to the cold light of rationality; they also allow themselves to reconsider their rational decisions when drunk. They seem to realize that drunkenness brings an insight that reason lacks.

Encountering uncertainty

Solving a problem means doing something. And all our actions have consequences, some of which are unpredictable.

Solving a problem, then, is always an encounter with uncertainty. Indeed, if the outcome of our solution were completely certain, there would be no need to decide what to do.

Extremely well-structured problems reduce the potential for uncertainty almost to zero. A puzzle will have usually one unambiguous answer; a plan will have a single, predictable outcome. When we follow a tried-and-tested recipe, we know that the food will be precisely what we expect it to be.

Uncertainty increases as a problem becomes less well structured. With a headache or a dream, the effects of our solution will be less certain. We'll have to consider the potential consequences of our action.

We'll need to decide what to do.

Herodotus' Persians teach us that the wise decision acknowledges two complementary approaches. What the Persians call 'sober' and 'drunken', we might call rational and intuitive. We've seen both at work throughout this book.

Each approach brings different skills to our decisions. Rationality involves planning, forecasting and analysing risk; intuition emphasizes reflection, insight and imagination. Rationality seeks to eliminate surprise; intuition, as we've seen, is always looking out for surprises – and trying to learn from them.

The two approaches can also help us understand how our decision affects others. Rationality analyses the stakeholders involved, to reduce their resistance or engage them as allies. But intuition gives us the insight to see our decision from their perspective. And, as Helga Drummond points out in *The Art of Decision Making*:

"Experience suggests that there are no good or bad decisions as such. More specifically, decisions succeed or fail according to whether they command support."

And where rationality scores over irrationality in its use of logic and patient analysis, intuition has one quality that trumps all rationality's powers of reasoning.

That quality is *the desire to act.*

We may regret deciding impetuously, without cool rational reflection; but a well-considered decision without the fire of passion to spur it on may never happen.

Biases and heuristics: shortcuts in intuitive problem-solving

Intuitive problem-solving uses shortcuts to interpret a situation and decide what to do. Scientists refer to these mental short-cuts as *biases* and *heuristics*. Biases are systematic tendencies to perceive reality in distorted ways; heuristics, as we've already seen in Chapter 6, are 'rules of thumb', systematic methods that sit halfway between a hunch and a formula.

Both biases and heuristics are usually seen as cognitive flaws. Biases distort our perception; heuristics limit our powers of judgement. And because both are unconscious, they're often seen as dangerous – as threats to our ability to solve problems well and decide wisely.

The idea of cognitive bias was first developed by Daniel Kahnemann and Amos Tversky in the 1970s. Since then, psychologists have compiled an ever-growing list of biases. (Wikipedia, at the time of writing, lists no fewer than 106.)

Here are a few of the most common.

Confirmation bias

Confirmation bias leads us to ignore evidence that contradicts our mental models. Faced with a new situation, we recognize what's familiar and ignore what's new; we see the similarities and ignore the differences. Faced with familiar symptoms, for example, a doctor may diagnose the most familiar disease and ignore the possibility of a rarer, more serious condition. Choosing between potential employees, we're likely to choose people who seem to be like us. Confirmation bias can be the source of prejudice.

The saliency effect

A variation of confirmation bias is the saliency effect, in which vivid or striking information becomes the benchmark by which we judge new information.

Sometimes we can become hypnotized by information that dazzles us. Information that's sufficiently vivid or salient can blind us to other, relatively dull, information: results of controlled surveys, trend analysis, and so on. The newspaper stories about people who win vast sums in a lottery create a saliency effect that blinds us to the very low statistical probability of winning. And so we hand over our money, again.

Anchoring

In novel situations, or ones where information is limited, we value early information more than later information. We *anchor* our decision to the information we receive first.

Some instances of anchoring are ridiculously simple. For example, if I described someone to you as 'intelligent, industrious, impulsive, critical, stubborn and envious', you are more likely to form a positive impression of that person than if I gave you the same descriptive words in reverse order.

Three types of anchoring are common in business decisions:

1. **The unchallenged guess.** A team proposing a capital investment project, for example, might simply guess the cost of an important component or resource – a guess that goes unchallenged by the management team.

2. **The extrapolation from the past.** We cannot believe that what has been happening so far won't simply continue. Analysts frequently seek to persuade investors to buy or sell a stock by showing a graph of a company's recent performance and extrapolating. That dotted line on the graph simply continues in the direction of the line indicating past performance. We've all read: 'Past performance is no guarantee of future results'. Anchoring is the bias that helps us ignore that self-evident truth and chase the money.

3. **The ruse.** Haggling is a prime example of deliberate, manipulative anchoring. An important element in negotiating, for example, is the anchoring by which one side attempts to influence the movements of the other side. Research suggests that a seller setting a high price will drag the buyer's response upwards: they've set an 'anchor' that the buyer finds hard to resist.

Loss aversion

We would rather avoid loss than make a gain. Imagine being asked whether you would prefer not to pay a £5 surcharge rather than receive a £5 discount. Most consumers would prefer to avoid paying the surcharge than given the discount – despite the fact that the overall effect on the price is the same.

Loss aversion makes us overly cautious in our attitude to risk. Because we prefer avoiding a loss to making a gain, we may prefer to avoid risk on the basis of what we might lose, rather than manage it in the hope of gaining a benefit.

Loss aversion may also explain …

The sunk cost effect

When considering whether to invest new resources or effort in a project, we should disregard past expenditures that don't affect future costs or revenues. But we don't. We find the idea that we've wasted the earlier investment too painful.

Pulling the plug on a huge project may be almost impossible because managers cannot bear to sacrifice the sunk costs. The British and French governments refused to cancel the Concorde project in the 1960s, even after it became clear that the aircraft could never recoup its investment costs. They were forced to 'throw good money after bad' because the alternative – having to admit that the investment was hopeless and the resources wasted – was political suicide.

Can we overcome our biases?

What should be our attitude to these biases and heuristics? Are we at their mercy? Is there nothing we can do to overcome the cognitive flaws that riddle our brains?

Daniel Kahnemann professes himself pessimistic. 'Knowing you have biases', he has written, 'is not enough to help you overcome them. You may accept that you have biases, but you cannot eliminate them in yourself.' He does think, however, that we can help others correct their biases. 'I am not very optimistic about people's ability to change the way they think', he says in a recent interview with the British magazine *New Scientist*, 'but I am fairly optimistic about their ability to detect the mistakes of others.'

From this perspective, our best hope in deciding more wisely would be to ask others for their help. Not bad advice.

What to do

The sceptic's checklist

Daniel Kahnemann suggests that all business decisions should be submitted to an external reviewer who systematically submits the idea to objective critique. Here's an adapted version of Kahnemann's 12-point checklist: when you've found a solution to a problem, hand this to a colleague and invite them to assess your idea by asking you these questions:

1 Where are you being driven by self-interest?

2 Have you fallen in love with your solution?

3 Has anyone criticized your solution yet?

4 Are you justifying your solution by comparing it to a notably successful past solution? If so, how do the two solutions differ?

5 Give me at least two credible alternatives to your solution.

6 If you had to make this decision again in a year's time, what information would you want? Can you get more of that information now?

7 Where have the numbers come from?

8 Are you being hypnotized by vivid or spectacular information, or by a charismatic personality?

9 Are you relying too much on past decisions to structure this solution?

10 Are you being overly optimistic in your projections?

11 What's the worst case scenario? Find a worse one.

12 Are you being overly cautious?

Optimism: the natural reality check

Maybe biases aren't always damaging. It seems that intuitive problem-solving has one particular bias that actually helps us learn from our mistakes.

It is known as the optimism bias.

We display the optimism bias whenever we expect our actions to be successful. Most gamblers expect to win. Most newly-weds believe their marriages will last longer than average. When was the last time you did something expecting to fail?

The optimism bias causes numerous problems. It can make us ignore the need for preventive healthcare or financial prudence; it can make us overestimate a project's benefits and underestimate its costs.

But optimism may also be beneficial. It may actually help us decide more wisely.

Tali Sharot, a neuroscientist who has studied the optimism bias, thinks that optimism helps us learn. Her research suggests that when we perform a task and optimistically expect success, a negative outcome triggers activity in our neocortex: our surprise makes us want to find out why our optimism was misplaced. Pessimism, in contrast, finds failure unsurprising and triggers no such activity.

Sharot's conclusion? Optimism makes us more sensitive to surprises. As she wrote in the *Observer*:

"A brain that doesn't expect good results lacks a signal telling it, 'Take notice – wrong answer!' These brains will fail to learn from their mistakes and are less likely to improve over time.**"**

Optimism gives us a natural reality check. Expecting positive outcomes helps us learn from our mistakes.

But only, of course, if we allow ourselves to make the mistakes in the first place.

How do we become more optimistic about our decisions? By making our solutions more feasible. And to do that, we need to enlist the help of rational problem-solving.

Building feasibility

Checklists are essential tools in rational problem-solving. They help us to think more systematically, navigate complex information more easily and keep our focus on our intended outcome. They also act as counterweights to any intuitive biases that may be influencing our thinking.

The business case checklist

Whether we're solving a business or a domestic problem, we need to know that our solution is for the greater good. Will this solution benefit our family, our community, our customers or our organization? The business case checklist will help you distinguish the really useful solutions from the ones that merely make you feel good.

Fill in the list on the following pages and don't be tempted to miss a box. When you've completed this checklist, your solution will be more vivid and detailed in your mind.

The business case checklist
What need is your solution addressing?
What outcomes are you aiming for?
What are the expected benefits?
Who will this solution benefit?
What key actions will you take to implement this solution? (Choose no more than six.) 1 2 3 4 5 6

▶

What is your deadline?

What resources do you need that you don't have? (Include a budget if necessary.)

What support will you need? (And where will you find it?)

Who are your stakeholders?

What will be the impact if you do not take any action?

What key behaviours and skills will need to be put into practice to achieve the desired result? (Include all the skills you might not currently have.)

What internal/external barriers do you see that could stop you being successful?

Solution effect analysis: managing risk

All decisions involve risk. Our action will have consequences; and we can't know, unless we're working with a completely closed system, exactly what those consequences will be.

We're dealing, then, with probability. We may see some consequences as certain (100% probability) and others as completely unlikely (0% probability). Most consequences will be harder to quantify. That doesn't mean, however, that we shouldn't try. Quantifying risk, however approximately, must be better than simply ignoring it.

We can make two basic calculations of probability:

1. the probability of success; and
2. the balance of risk and reward.

Estimating the probability of success itself means asking two questions:

1. What could go wrong?
2. How likely is it to happen?

Look for the factors outside your circle of influence that may affect the success of your decision. A decision that relies for its success on an upturn in the market or a change in the weather is highly risky.

How does contemplating failure help increase our optimism? Perhaps you'll feel *more* optimistic about your decision if you can quantify the probability of failure – and then reduce it.

Solution effect analysis (SEA) tests a decision and identifies its effects. It will help you to:

- see whether the decision will actually solve the problem you want to solve;
- compare the effects of different courses of action;
- check that your action doesn't create new problems; and
- identify the actions you need to take to implement your decision successfully.

Solution effect analysis (SEA)

1 Define the course of action you intend to take.

2 Identify the major categories within which you want to assess the effects of the action. It's important to choose these categories carefully.

3 Explore the potential effects of the decision within each category. Take your time. Allow your mind to work out the effects within each area. If one category becomes overloaded, the part of your plan of action relating to that area may need rethinking.

4 Analyse the effects. Highlight the effects that need immediate attention, and also any linkages between effects. Above all, don't ignore any adverse effects or new problems. You may need to balance the difficulties of implementing your decision against the benefits of seeing it through.

SEA usually benefits from being drawn as a diagram (see Figure 10.1). Draw it exactly as you would an Ishikawa or fishbone diagram, placing the decision on the left-hand side of a large sheet of paper and drawing a horizontal line from it. Add stems at 45 degrees for each major category. Add further stems for the potential effects within each category.

Analysis paralysis and its antidote

The danger with checklists, of course, is that they can seduce us into endless analysis and stop us from doing anything.

Rational thinking demands knowledge in order to be effective. One of the mantras of rational problem-solving is that the more we know about a problem, the better placed we'll be to solve it. The temptation, then, is to feed our rationality with more and more information. And here, paradoxically, is rationality's hidden weakness: the search for complete knowledge.

For the truth is that we *always* have to decide with inadequate knowledge. We can never know whether, or when, new information will arrive; we always have to make the best use of the information we have at the time.

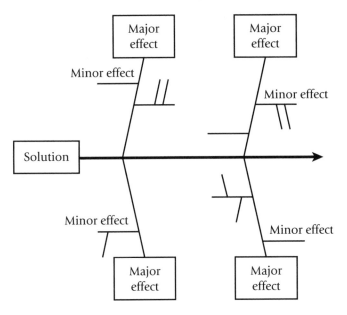

Figure 10.1 An SEA diagram

It's this paradox – the demand for more information and the inability ever to have complete knowledge – that can cause analysis paralysis.

Assessing opportunity cost

Opportunity cost is the sacrifice we make to gain or achieve something else of value. Analysis paralysis occurs when the opportunity cost of analysis exceeds the benefits that we can gain from deciding what to do.

We are more prone to analysis paralysis when we perceive the opportunity cost of a decision to be high. We're less likely to succumb to analysis paralysis when choosing a new brand of washing powder than when choosing a new house, job or partner as the opportunity costs are much lower.

The key question to ask is: at what point does the opportunity cost of analyzing a problem exceed the benefit of making a decision?

How do we know when to stop analyzing and take action?

What to do

Do you sometimes suffer from analysis paralysis?

You might be prone to analysis paralysis if your problem-solving profile strongly favours the Analyst or Designer styles. The Analyst style may tend to demand more and more information before taking action; the Designer style may remain unhappy with a solution unless it's aesthetically perfect.

If you think you may be analyzing a problem too deeply, take time out to exercise your Explorer or Engineer styles. Ask yourself some of these questions and run some more thought experiments.

Explorer

- What is this problem like? (Find an analogy in another field. How does it get solved in that field?)

- How would a professional of a different kind solve this problem? (Are you a financial analyst? Imagine how a plumber might solve your problem. Are you a lawyer? Imagine how a doctor might solve the problem.)

- What's the reverse of this problem? (Or: imagine deciding to do the opposite ...)

Engineer

- Imagine that this is an emergency. If you had to fix this problem right now, with only two minutes to spare, what would you do?

- What needs mending? Focus on one element of the problem that you can put right.

- What about compromising? What about a 'quick fix'? Where could you apply a 'sticking plaster' to the problem? What would be the consequences of a 'quick fix'?

Satisficing: an antidote to analysis paralysis

Imagine choosing a new house. You might start by drawing up a list of criteria and judging each house against the list, but there will come a point where the opportunity cost of comparing and contrasting houses outweighs the benefits of choosing. At that point, you'll look for a house that's satisfactory rather than perfect.

This decision is an example of what researchers call 'satisficing': finding a solution that meets our criteria for adequacy. (The word was coined by Herbert Simon in the 1950s.) Satisficing means abandoning the search for the best solution, and opting instead for the *first reasonable solution*.

A children's riddle

Why are things always in the last place you look for them? Because you stop looking when you find them.

In particular, we might satisfice when we lack:

- information; or
- the ability to process information.

And we may lack the ability to process information for all sorts of reasons:

- We may have too little or too much information.
- The information may be incomplete or inaccurate.
- We may lack the resources or the skill to process the information.
- We might have a lot of decisions to make.
- We may simply not have the time to analyse the situation adequately. In an emergency, for example, satisficing may be the only option.

To break out of analysis paralysis, start satisficing.

What to do

I'll tell you what I want: drawing up a selection matrix

One way to get yourself satisficing is to draw up a list of your key criteria of choice. Rather than analyzing all the information about all the options, identify what you're looking for in a solution and find the first option that meets those criteria. It may not be the best one, but how much effort and resource would become opportunity cost finding a better one?

Time to reach for your spreadsheet:

1 Gather the options facing you and give each a column. Make one option a default option: often it's the 'do nothing' or 'stay as I am' choice. That choice is rated zero for all criteria.

2 Identify the criteria by which you'll judge each option. Give each a row on your spreadsheet.

3 Give each option a rating for each criterion: 1, 0, or –1, depending on whether that option is better, equivalent or worse than the status quo.

4 If you judge some criteria to be more important than others, weight them accordingly. Don't adjust too strongly.

5 What comes out as the best choice? Do you feel good about that choice? If so, make your choice.

6 If you don't feel good about what the spreadsheet tells you, consider your list of criteria and your weighting.

It's clear that a selection matrix is only as objective as our choices of criteria. Notice also that it can't accommodate *combinations* of criteria. Imagine drawing up a selection matrix to choose a mobile phone: you might weight a combination of web access and high-performance camera higher than the combined weightings you gave to each individual feature.

Your final decision may still be intuitive. But the selection matrix has at least guided your options and given your intuition something more to work with – or ignore!

A selection matrix may help you break your analysis paralysis, but it has its limitations. For example, it applies rationality to a situation where rationality may be breaking down. How many times have we listed criteria for choice in a tricky situation, only to massage them towards the choice that we really want to make?

Satisficing, it seems, can't be pinned down rationally. It's largely an intuitive technique, and that may be its greatest value. Just as checklists and other tools of rationality can help to balance the excesses of intuitive bias, so satisficing may come to our aid when rationality tips over into analysis paralysis.

Gary Klein, a cognitive psychologist, has studied the way people make decisions in difficult or stressful situations. He noticed that fire crew commanders, for example, faced with a serious blaze, rarely pursued the textbook decision-making protocol. Instead, they satisfice. As he explained in a *Fast Company* interview:

❝If everything works out okay, the commanders stick with their choice. But if they discover unintended consequences that could get them into trouble, they discard that solution and look for another one. They might run through several choices, but they never compare one option with another. They rapidly evaluate each choice on its own merits, even if they cycle through several possibilities. They don't need the best solution. They just need the one that works.**❞**

(Which sounds strikingly similar to the opportunity-led problem solving we explored in Chapter 8.)

Satisficing seems to work by pattern-matching. Over time, we build up a collection of experiences; faced with a new situation, we run a super-rapid search through the database to find the pattern that matches. As soon as satisficing makes a match, it kicks into action.

How do we assemble these invaluable mental pattern catalogues? Through experience. Or rather: by having experiences.

In other words, an expert satisficer is marked out from a novice by their experiences. Satisficing relies on 'tacit knowledge': the kind of knowledge that can't be codified in lists or instruction manuals. We gain tacit knowledge only from doing things and learning from them. Weighing options may make sense if we're new to decision-making in a particular area, but the way to improve our satisficing skills is to have more experiences.

So the best thing to do, if you want to improve your decision-making skills, might be to make as many decisions as possible.

Engagement: delaying the point of no return

Making a decision demands courage – no matter how much preparation, testing and calculating we've done. How can we develop courage?

One way is to gain more control over the situation. Preparation, planning and all the other tools and techniques of rational problem-solving can help us confront our fears more easily. Training to sky-dive, and knowing that you're wearing a highly effective parachute, may not dispel your terror at leaping from an aircraft at 20,000 feet – but it may reduce your fear sufficiently to allow you to jump.

Another way to become more courageous is to build *reversibility* into a decision, so that we can somehow manage the point of no return. And we have, in fact, invented an excellent practice to do just that.

It's called 'getting engaged'.

When a couple decide to marry, they often announce their engagement. It's a useful institution: the couple can test their decision in public and delay making the final commitment. We can transfer the idea of marital engagement to other activities. A pilot scheme, a trial run or a survey, like an engagement, allow us to test our decision before reaching the point of no return.

❝A good decision made today is generally better than a good decision made in a few weeks' time. Be really clear about accountability; about who has to make that decision. Make the decision; make it quickly; and make sure you can reverse it if it goes wrong.❞
                                    Ian Livingston, Group CEO, British Telecom

In brief

Solving a problem is always an encounter with uncertainty. Uncertainty increases as a problem becomes less well structured. A wise decision involves both rationality and intuition.

Rationality tends to be slow; intuition tends to be fast. Rational decision-making involves logic, planning, forecasting, analysing risk and eliminating surprise; intuitive decision-making emphasizes desire, reflection, insight imagination and the search for surprises.

Rationality analyses the stakeholders involved in implementing a decision; intuition imagines the effects of the solution from the stakeholders' perspectives.

Intuitive problem-solving uses biases and heuristics to interpret a situation and decide what to do. These are usually seen as cognitive flaws: biases distort our perception; heuristics limit our powers of judgement. We may not be able to see the biases affecting our own decisions, but we can ask others to point them out to us.

The optimism bias may help us make better decisions. Optimism – when it generates surprise – provides us with a natural reality check. It enables us to learn more effectively when we're surprised by unexpected outcomes.

We can become more optimistic about our decisions by making our solutions more feasible. Checklists are one way to build feasibility into our decisions.

Rationality's thirst for knowledge can lead to analysis paralysis, in which the opportunity cost of analysis exceeds the benefits that we can gain from deciding what to do.

We can escape analysis paralysis by satisficing: abandoning the search for the best solution, and opting instead for the *first reasonable solution*. The best way to satisfice is to build up a database of experiences that intuition can draw on.

▶

Decision-making demands courage. We can become more courageous by preparing fully and by building *reversibility* into a decision. All decisions are engagements with an evolving, ever-changing reality; thinking about a problem and solving it can never truly be separated.

Chapter

11

Towards collaboration: solving problems with other people

Solving problems is tricky enough when we're working on our own. It can become even more difficult if we're trying to solve a problem with other people.

This chapter won't be a lengthy discussion about all the inter-personal skills involved in working in groups. (If you'd like to discover more about these skills, my book *How to Manage Meetings* includes a chapter on how groups work.) Instead, we'll explore here how to use the problem-solving tools and techniques we've already discovered to collaborate with others.

Collaborative problem-solving must begin and end with decisions about who owns the problem. The key questions, in order, are:

1. Who owns the problem?
2. Who else is involved? Who are the stakeholders?
3. How will the stakeholders relate to the problem-owner?
4. How will the stakeholders and the problem-owner work together?
5. Who owns the solution?

To answer the first question, look back at our exploration of ownership in Chapter 4.

In this chapter, we shall assume that the problem-owner is you.

Disconnects: solutions need owners, too

Solutions in organizations often fail because nobody owns them. A solution becomes a victim to 'disconnects', which can occur when the two stages of problem-solving – defining the problem and constructing a solution – become separated. (The concept of disconnects is another of Fred Nickols' brainchildren.)

Some disconnects are vertical. Senior management decides to simplify a process; middle management analyses the existing process and the criteria for improving it, then designs a new process; finally, line management tries to implement the new process, tweaking it to make it fit all the contingencies of everyday working – and all too often the new process becomes more complicated than the old one.

But disconnects can also occur laterally. Relationships between customers and suppliers, or between clients and consultants, can become disconnected.

Whenever you hear the words, 'but that's not what I wanted', you're probably hearing evidence of a lateral disconnect. Disconnects often occur, for example, between IT departments and users. Users complain that IT has produced a solution that doesn't do what users want; the boffins retort that the brief was unclear; and so on, round and round. (Agile Software Development, which we met in Chapter 8, is a response to this very problem.)

According to Fred Nickols:

"The obvious response to disconnects is to provide continuity. Sooner or later, the whole thing must pass through and fit in one brain; if not, it ain't gonna work, 'cause no one understands it from end to end."

In other words: one person must take ownership of the solution.

Who are the stakeholders?

Stakeholders are the people who have both an interest in the solution and the power to influence our problem-solving work. You might not welcome the fact that other people have a stake in your problem: we saw in Chapter 7 that problems can become wicked as more and more people become involved. But it's important to view the stakeholders, not as potential troublemakers but as a valuable resource.

- You can use stakeholders' experience, expertise and resources to help you solve the problem.
- Involving them will increase the likelihood that they will support you and collaborate with you.

The first step in your stakeholder analysis is to brainstorm who your stakeholders are. Who is affected by the problem? Who has contributed to it? Who has power to influence the situation or to help you make a solution happen?

What to do

One way to cover all the stakeholders is the 'nine Cs' checklist, originally drawn up by the National Health Service:

1 **Commissioners:** those that pay you to do things.

2 **Customers:** those who buy your products or services.

3 **Collaborators:** the people you work with to develop and deliver your products or services.

4 **Contributors:** those who provide raw materials or knowledge.

5 **Channels:** the marketers and distributors with a route to your customers.

6 **Commentators:** whose opinions about you are heard or seen by customers and others.

7 **Consumers:** the people served by your customers.

8 **Champions:** those who can sponsor, promote and support your efforts.

9 **Competitors:** the people working in the same area who offer similar or alternative services.

You may identify both organizations and individuals as stakeholders, but you can only deal with people. Make sure that you identify the appropriate individual stakeholders within a stakeholder organization.

▶

Stakeholder analysis

Once you have decided who owns the problem, map out the problem's **stakeholders**: everyone who has a stake in the problem, the solution and any possible consequences.

You could map stakeholders on a large piece of flipchart paper, with those most affected or involved near the centre and others at varying distances from the centre.

You can also link stakeholders whose interests are related.

How will the stakeholders relate to you (and the problem)?

You now have a list of stakeholders who are affected by the problem. Some will have power to help or hinder you; some will have an interest in generating a solution, while others will not. Your manager, for example, probably has power to influence what you do, and may have high interest in generating a solution. A customer may have very high interest in generating a solution, but little obvious power in your organization.

Map out your stakeholders on a power/interest grid, to work out how you will involve them in your problem-solving efforts.

	Communicate	Collaborate
High power	These are the opinion-formers. Keep them informed about what you're doing; review your analysis of their position regularly.	Key stakeholders who should be fully engaged as partners in the problem-solving process.
	Consider	Consult
Low power	Do little with these people but keep an eye on them. Their interest or power may rise if circumstances change.	Increase their influence by asking them for their opinions: interviews, surveys, focus groups. They may become consultants in all but name.
	Low interest	*High interest*

Your working methods will differ with each of these four groups. With the collaborators, you are likely to set up problem-solving meetings, and these need to be well managed.

What groups need to solve problems

We think differently when we think in a group. All too often, in fact, we think less effectively when others are involved. But group problem-solving can work extremely well – if it follows some basic disciplines.

An effective problem-solving group:

- agrees its goal;
- understands people's roles in the team;
- has an agreed process for tackling the problem;
- uses deliberate techniques to discipline its thinking;
- is ready to adapt the process as the need arises;
- closely monitors its own behaviour;
- shares information; and
- has a leader who adapts their style to the needs of the problem and the group.

Allocating roles

The key roles in a problem-solving group are:

- the problem-owner;
- thinking consultants; and
- a process leader.

And it's a good idea to allocate these three roles to different people. In particular, the problem-owner and the process leader should be two different people. Why?

1. **We confuse conversation about the task with conversation about process.** We identify thoughts with people. We talk in code. We use conversation to express loyalties or alliances, to bid for power, to protect our position or sense of self-worth. We persist in old conventions or habits of conversation to feel more comfortable.

2. **We fail to manage the structure of the conversation.** A well-managed conversation will begin with clear objectives and end with clear actions. Many conversations have unclear agendas (or hidden agendas); others are combinations of several conversations at once. We allow our conversations to ramble, to get stuck, to be hijacked or stifled. Because the behavioural or 'political' aspects of conversation are so powerful, we find it difficult to influence the course of conversations productively – particularly in a meeting, when a group of people are involved.

The process leader will help the group discipline its thinking, apply thinking tools more effectively and keep the conversation on track. That's a full-time task. It makes sense, therefore, that the process leader and the problem-solver should be different people.

Among the thinking consultants, have as rich a mix as possible of the four problem-solving styles: Analyst, Explorer, Engineer and Designer. Use the skills of each style as appropriate at different times in the problem-solving process, and for different types of problem.

Group problem-solving should do two things:

1. **Distinguish ideas from people.** The quality of a group's thinking often suffers because ideas become confused with the people holding them. Making ideas the property of the group allows us to process them with less potential for conflict.

2. **Focus attention.** The group should be thinking together: about the same issue, and in the same way. Simply using the same words may not be sufficient; a single word can have multiple connotations, depending on who's using it. We should all be clearly focused on the same area of concern; and we should know what *kind* of thinking we are doing at any point.

Distinguishing ideas from people

Group problem-solving is always vulnerable to conflict. When we think in a group, we easily confuse an idea with the person holding it. Attacking an idea means attacking the person. Conflict nearly always includes emotional arousal, which, as we've seen in Chapter 2, limits our ability to think rationally – or, indeed, intuitively.

We can encounter four main types of conflict in group problem-solving.

1. *Critical thinking.*

   Critical thinking always seeks what's wrong with an idea. Simply to find fault is a very limited way of assessing an idea's value. It can also easily sound like a criticism of the idea-holder.

2. *Ego thinking.*

   'I am my idea.' Once we identify ourselves with ideas, they become **opinions**. We are so used to opinions that we easily mistake them for the truth. Whenever you hear the word 'fact' in a meeting, you can be almost certain that somebody is voicing an opinion.

3. *Political thinking.*

   When ideas become opinions, voicing an idea becomes a political act. To attack an idea is to attack its sponsor; to support it is to create an alliance. We use conversation to create 'power bases' and undermine 'opponents', manipulate ideas, send up smoke screens, foment dissent or rumour.

4. *Rigid thinking.*

   Adversarial thinking sets ideas against each other. If an idea is to survive the battle, it must become rigid. A debate is a conflict of rigid ideas. Debate is probably the only organized conversation we know. It is also the least effective.

The process leader can manage these different forms of conflict by asking the group questions:

- To manage **critical thinking**, ask for positive responses to an idea: 'What's good about this idea?'.
- To manage **ego thinking**, ask for evidence to support opinions. Ask: 'In what circumstances?'. Evaluate ideas for their relevance to objectives.

- To manage **political thinking**, invite the whole group to think systematically. Ask for positive and negative responses to an idea in order. Develop this approach by using tools such as SWOT analysis (strengths, weaknesses, opportunities and threats), asking the group to concentrate on one aspect at a time.

- To manage **rigid thinking**, ask: 'What if?'. Look deliberately for the assumptions behind ideas and challenge them. Ask how the matter would look from a radically different perspective. Turn ideas upside down and see what happens.

Managing the process

Another way to discipline the group's thinking is to focus on the problem-solving process itself.

One basic question to ask is: are we doing Stage 1 or Stage 2 thinking? In other words, are we seeking to understand the problem or generate a solution?

- Stage 1 thinking typically involves analyzing and exploring the problem.

- Stage 2 thinking typically involves engineering or designing a solution.

Simply keeping a group focused on one stage of the problem-solving process can be a challenge. You could begin by using the problem matrix (in Chapter 5) to help the group categorize and define the problem.

Making our thinking visible

Stage 1 thinking is always about being able to *see* a problem more clearly, more deeply or more imaginatively. A group working on a problem will always benefit from a shared visual representation of the problem – especially if they can create it themselves.

Many techniques and technologies have appeared over the years to help groups visualize their thinking. Yet it's surprising how many groups try to work together with no visual element whatsoever. Some meeting rooms are equipped with white boards – many of which are now interactive – or flipcharts.

Lo-tech tools such as sticky notes can be hugely effective. The key is to be able to use a range of techniques with these tools, to help us visualize our ideas.

Two technologies in particular have proved enormously successful in making use of our capacity to think visually. Both claim not merely to represent our thinking more effectively, but actually to help us think more creatively. And neither of them uses electricity!

Mind maps

Mind maps are diagrams representing words, ideas, tasks, or other items linked to and arranged around a central key word or idea. We can use mind maps to generate, structure and classify ideas, as well as the connections between them.

Mind maps are closely associated with Tony Buzan. In *The Mind Map Book*, Buzan offers four principles for creating them:

1. **Use emphasis.** Always use a central image. Use images throughout the map, using three or more colours. Give your images dimensions, and vary the size of printing, lines and images.
2. **Use association.** Draw arrows, colours and codes to connect elements within the map.
3. **Be clear.** Use sheets of paper in 'landscape format' (the long side horizontal). Keep printing as upright as you can. Print key words on lines: only one word per line. Make line length equal to word length. Connect lines to other lines (no 'free-floating' lines). Make central lines thicker. Make images as clear as possible. Draw boundaries around branch outlines.
4. **Develop a personal style.** Each mind map you draw should be slightly more imaginative and beautiful than the last.

Rich pictures

Rich pictures are variants on mind maps that are particularly valuable in picturing a large-scale system such as an organization or network. Rich pictures grew out of Soft Systems Methodology (SSM), developed during the 1960s and 1970s by Peter Checkland and his students at Lancaster University.

Rich pictures are particularly powerful in mapping wicked problems. They help us map not only the obvious facts of a situation, but also abstract or emotional factors such as the social atmosphere among the actors. A rich picture represents what we know about a messy situation: the issues, the actors, the problems, processes, relationships, conflicts and motivations. Drawing a rich picture helps us to see not only the obvious facts about a situation, but the emotional and social factors underlying it. You can find plenty of examples on the internet.

How to draw a rich picture

Begin with a large sheet of paper and a lot of differently coloured pens. Draw what you see happening in the situation. Include everything that you perceive to be problematic or significant: emotions and relationships as well as organizational groupings. Use symbols and metaphors.

All rich pictures include three important components:

1 **Structure** refers to aspects of the work context that are slow to change. These might be things such as the organizational hierarchy of a firm, geographic localities, physical equipment, and so on. Most important, it includes all the people who will use or could conceivably be affected by the introduction of the new system.

2 **Process** refers to the transformations that occur in the process of the work. These transformations might be part of a flow of goods, documents or data.

3 **Concerns** capture people's motivations for participating in the situation. Different motivations create different perspectives on the situation. You might capture concerns in 'thought bubbles'; conflict between participants might be represented by a 'crossed swords' symbol; and so on.

Focusing on structure, process and concerns helps prevent the rich picture becoming overloaded with detail.

Brainstorming: helping groups solve problems?

In the past 50 years a whole industry has grown up devoted to developing and promoting group problem-solving techniques. Among the earliest is brainstorming, invented by Alex Osborn in the 1930s. Osborn offers four basic rules for brainstorming.

Alex Osborn's four rules of brainstorming

1 *Criticism is ruled out.* Ideas are to be judged later, not during the session.

2 *'Freewheeling' is welcome.* The wilder the idea, the better. It's easier to tame down than to think up.

3 *We want more!* The more ideas, the more the likelihood of a good new one.

4 *Combine and improve.* As well as contributing ideas, team members should suggest ways of improving, combining, or varying others' ideas.

Beyond these simple rules, Osborn emphasizes the importance of:

● getting going – not waiting for inspiration to strike;

● focusing – on the objective of the session, what we want to achieve;

● attention – of the whole team to one kind of thinking at a time;

● concentration – sticking at it, refusing to give up if no ideas come.

In the decades since Osborn published his ideas in his book, *Applied Imagination*, a good deal of research has investigated whether brainstorming does indeed help groups to generate creative ideas. The results have been ambiguous: groups don't seem to be as effective as individuals at generating ideas, though they do seem to be able to evaluate and develop ideas more powerfully.

These findings are hardly surprising. An idea can only ever form in a single mind. Groups in themselves cannot generate ideas. A brainstorming session works best when it provides the environment for individuals to have ideas and voice them.

Developing your brainstorming skills

Brainstorming may benefit from a few simple additional guidelines to Osborn's original four principles.

Separate individual from group brainstorming. Ask people to generate ideas individually to begin the process. Gather them anonymously to encourage the wilder ideas to surface and counter any politics or inhibitions in the team. Then use group brainstorming to group the ideas, build on them, combine them, vary them, develop them and transform them.

Set targets. The discipline of 'scoring' can produce more ideas and help crazier ideas to surface. A target of between 50 and 100 ideas in 10 minutes is not unreasonable for a competent team of about seven people.

Vary the session's structure. Change the way the session runs by:

- briefing the team with the problem a day beforehand, to allow for private musing and 'sleeping on the problem';
- beginning the session with a warm-up exercise, unrelated to the task in hand;
- taking breaks between techniques, to allow people's minds to relax and discover new ideas.

Running a 'how to' session

A 'how to' session is a powerful variant on brainstorming.

Begin by identifying the problem-owner and asking them to define the problem as a 'how to' statement. They should present the problem to the group in no more than a few minutes.

What to do

How to present a 'how to' statement

If you are the problem-owner, use this checklist to help you talk briefly about the problem.

How to:

....

- **Background.** How has the task come about? Why does it need to be done? What is the context?

- **Ownership.** Why are you involved? Where does it hurt? How does it affect you personally? What motivates you to find a solution?

- **Past efforts.** What has already been tried or considered? By whom? Do any solutions already exist? Why are they unsatisfactory?

- **Power to act.** What are you in a position to do? What are you willing to do? What constraints are you operating within? Who else is involved? How?

- **Big wish.** If miracles could happen, what would you ask for? What's your vision for the future?

The group leader may need to remove the problem-owner from the group after presenting the problem. If they stay in the group, appoint someone to manage the problem-owner's behaviour so that they don't stifle the group's thinking with operational objections and idea killers.

Now ask the group to generate as many new 'how to' statements as possible. (Look back at Chapter 8 for details.) Record the new 'how to' statements on sticky notes, so that the group can cluster them into themes. Ask the group to create clusters of 'how to' statements that it can use to present its thinking to the problem-owner.

Invite the problem-owner to inspect the collection of 'how to' statements. Some of the 'how to' statements may strike them at once as feasible solutions and others as ideas for practical solutions. A third group might intrigue and excite them: they may feel that they would really like to do what the 'how to' suggests, and they don't know how. These are potentially the most interesting ideas, so ask the group to develop them further into ideas for solutions.

Developing solutions in group problem-solving

Groups are usually much better at evaluating and developing ideas than having them. A group problem-solving session can add real value by concentrating on working an idea into a feasible, practical course of action.

Use the business case checklist and solution effect analysis (SEA) that we looked at in Chapter 10.

Who owns the solution?

Once a group has been through a problem-solving process, it's critically important to establish who is going to make the solution happen.

Think back to Chapter 4: is the solution-owner taking responsibility for the solution, or are they energetically committed to implementing it? What can the group do to help transform the solution-owner's responsibility into real commitment? And how is the solution-owner proposing to make the solution work?

Asking someone to take responsibility for a solution

Taking responsibility for a solution, as we saw in Chapter 4, should be a free act. Simply telling someone to implement a solution is unlikely to guarantee a positive outcome. The best way to establish someone's ownership of a solution is to negotiate:

1. I ask you to do something by a certain time. I make it clear that this is a request, not an order.
2. You have four possible responses to this request:
   - You may accept.
   - You may decline.
   - You may commit to accept or decline later ('I'll let you know by . . .').
   - You may make a counter-offer ('No, but I can do ...').
3. With any response except the first, you and I must now negotiate until the contract is settled.
4. It's critical that the solution-owner understands the boundaries of their responsibility. (Use the six Ws as outlined in Chapter 4.)
5. The conversation should result in a promise: 'I shall do x for you by time y.'

Making solutions work

Solutions, as we know, are courses of action. They make change happen. And, as we also know, change introduces uncertainty, and uncertainty can provoke resistance – especially in the stakeholders who are affected by it. Think especially about the stakeholders who aren't in the 'collaborate' category: they probably haven't been closely involved in creating the solution, but they will feel its effects and may have to work with it.

As we saw in Chapter 4, resistance can be the result of procedures being disrupted and needs not being recognized. Success will come from *reducing* the resistance: recognizing that disruptions to procedures need to be navigated, and meeting needs wherever possible.

What to do

Some suggestions for transforming resistance into commitment

- Show people how the new solution connects to their current procedures. How will it make their work easier? What are you doing to make the transition as seamless and painless as possible?

- Demonstrate the value of the solution in contributing to everyone's success – and to the success of the organization.

- Communicate: clearly, honestly and consistently. And keep communicating.

- Give people opportunities to involve themselves in the solution, and to contribute ideas to improve it still further.

- As the owner of the solution, see yourself as a leader, enabling people to make the change happen, encouraging and inspiring them to success.

Force-field analysis

Force-field analysis develops the idea of resistance from the level of the individual to the level of the system. By representing a situation as a dynamic, open system, force-field analysis shows how a new solution can disrupt the balance of the system by exerting force in a certain direction. The inevitable result within the system will be resistance.

The system will only change if the resisting forces are weakened. Exerting more force for change will simply increase resistance.

Force-field analysis creates a simple, clear model of the forces supporting and opposing change (see Figure 11.1).

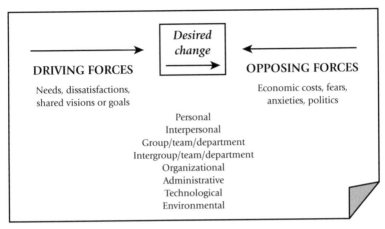

Figure 11.1 The forces supporting and opposing change

Take care to confine your analysis to an identifiable system: a team, a department, an organization, a partnership. Analyse the forces at work on the system – not on individuals within the system. Consider only those forces you can positively identify, not possible forces.

Identify the desired outcome or objective. As driving forces, look for:

- needs within the stakeholder group;
- shared dissatisfactions that the outcome will address; and
- shared visions of success.

As opposing forces, look for:

- economic costs; and
- psychological costs – fear, anxiety, political opposition, resistance to the change.

Address the opposing forces by creating constructed problems – 'how to' statements:

- What is the relative importance of the forces? Can you quantify them?
- Which forces can you influence immediately?
- To whom do you have immediate access?

- How ready is the system for change?
- How can you deal with the psychological costs of change?
- Where will you have to forge links between parts of the system to create change?
- What are the consequences on the system of failing to change?

In brief

Collaboration is founded on identifying both the problem-owner and the solution-owner.

Think of the problem's stakeholders as a valuable resource. List them and map them out on a power/interest grid.

An effective problem-solving group:

- agrees its goal;
- understands people's roles in the team;
- has an agreed process for tackling the problem;
- uses deliberate techniques to discipline its thinking;
- is ready to adapt the process as the need arises;
- closely monitors its own behaviour;
- shares information; and
- has a leader who adapts their style to the needs of the problem and the group.

The key roles in a problem-solving group are:

- the problem-owner;
- thinking consultants; and
- a process leader.

Process leaders can help by managing critical thinking, ego thinking, political thinking and rigid thinking when they arise. They can also help discipline the group's thinking by focusing on the problem-solving process.

Two technologies – mind maps and rich pictures – are useful to help the group visualize problems.

Brainstorming is a well-known problem-solving technique with four basic rules:

1 *Criticism is ruled out.* Ideas are to be judged later, not during the session.

2 *'Freewheeling' is welcome.* The wilder the idea, the better. It's easier to tame down than to think up.

▶

3 *We want more!* The more ideas, the more the likelihood of a good new one.

4 *Combine and improve.* As well as contributing ideas, team members should suggest ways of improving, combining or varying others' ideas.

We can improve the success of brainstorming sessions by:

- separating individual from group brainstorming;
- setting targets; and
- varying the session's structure.

A 'how to' session is a powerful kind of brainstorming meeting.

A group problem-solving session can add real value by concentrating on building a solution's feasibility. It's critically important to establish the solution-owner.

Solutions may provoke resistance among those affected by them. We can lower resistance by:

- showing people how the new solution connects to their current procedures;
- demonstrating the value of the solution in contributing to everyone's success;
- communicating clearly, honestly and consistently;
- giving people opportunities to involve themselves in the solution; and
- leading the implementation through enabling, encouraging and inspiring.

Force-field analysis helps us manage this resistance and lower it. It develops the idea of resistance from the level of the individual to the level of the system.

Afterword

We started out on this journey, in Chapter 1, by entering the space that opens up in our heads when we're stuck. Intuitive problem-solving is never stuck for something to do. Intuition matches a situation to a mental pattern and acts on it. When intuitive problem-solving breaks down – when we want to do something, but we don't know what to do – we can turn to rational problem-solving.

But in opening up that space between understanding a problem and generating a solution, we've separated the two parts of problem-solving that ought to remain together: thinking and doing. Throughout this book, we've discovered that success in solving problems means bringing these two stages closer. In Chapter 11 we sought to unite them, at the moment of deciding what to do. Thinking about a problem and solving it can never truly be separated.

Herodotus' Persians knew that a wise decision requires both rationality and intuition. The whole aim of problem-solving is to change a situation by doing something. Common sense might suggest that thinking precedes action: that problem-solving comes before solving the problem. Experience teaches us otherwise. In complex situations, there are no clear answers and no fixes – quick or otherwise. All our actions are engagements with an evolving, ever-changing reality, and the consequences of our actions can never be certain. And solving a problem will always teach us more about the problem we're trying to solve.

In the words of Karl Weick, an organizational theorist and professor at the University of Michigan: 'We think by acting.'

Stuckness shouldn't be avoided.
It's the psychic predecessor of all
real understanding.

Robert M. Pirsig, *Zen and the Art of
Motorcycle Maintenance*, Chapter 24

Index